GRENFELL OF LABRADOR

GRENFELL
of
LABRADOR

❖━❖━❖━❖━❖━❖━❖━❖━❖━

By George H. Pumphrey

ILLUSTRATED WITH PHOTOGRAPHS

DODD, MEAD & COMPANY
New York, 1959

Preface

ANYONE who writes about Sir Wilfred Grenfell must inevitably turn to his autobiography, *A Labrador Doctor,* as the main source of information. In this wonderful book, however, Sir Wilfred is so modest that we often find it difficult to piece together the vivid, lively character that guided his remarkable achievements in Labrador. The men and women who worked with him in the early days in Labrador and are still alive are now well on in years, but their memories of Sir Wilfred are as vivid as ever. I have written this book in order to introduce Sir Wilfred to boys and girls, so that they will later turn to his autobiography.

Sir Wilfred's inspiration is still remarkably strong, and the work in Labrador could not carry on without the doctors, nurses, teachers, and other helpers who go out to his Mission each year. Although circumstances are much changed since Sir Wilfred's early days, help for the people of Labrador is still urgently needed.

I have to thank Miss Betty Seabrook, the Secretary of the Grenfell Association of Great Britain and Ireland, for her invaluable help with information and pictures for this book. All the illustrations are the copyright of the Association and are reproduced with their kind permission. I have also to thank the Association for their permission to reproduce an extract from a report (1947) by Sir Henry Richards; the Rev. Henry Gordon for an extract from a speech made by him in 1956; Mr. A. M. Daryl Grenfell for an extract from the Mostyn House School magazine, *The Griffin;* the Editor for an extract from an article by Miss Patricia Knapp in the International Grenfell Association magazine, *Among the Deep Sea Fishers;* and Messrs. Christy and Moore, Ltd. for extracts from *A Labrador Doctor* (Hodder and Stoughton), by Sir Wilfred Grenfell.

G.H.P.

Contents

Illustrations

GRENFELL OF LABRADOR

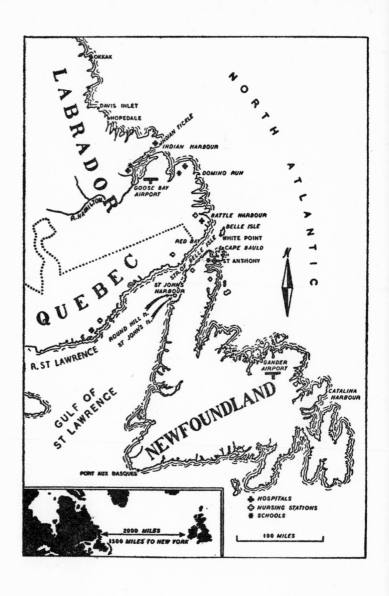

1

◆◆◆◆◆◆◆◆◆◆◆◆◆◆◆

Wilfred Grenfell's Boyhood

WILFRED GRENFELL was born in 1865 at Parkgate, a
little fishing village on the Cheshire shore of the river
Dee.

His father was the headmaster and owner of Mostyn
House, a boarding-school whose large white buildings
still dominate the sea-front at Parkgate.

Wilfred was the second of four brothers. Maurice, the
third brother, died when he was seven, and the fourth,
Cecil, was too young to be a real companion for the older
boys. Although Algernon, the eldest brother, and Wilfred did not spend a great deal of time together, their
worst escapades were usually carried out in each other's
company.

Algernon certainly seems to have been something of
a schoolmaster's nightmare. One of his most spectacular
scrapes took place at his public school, where he used
phosphorus, taken from the laboratory, to draw lu-

minous ghosts on the dormitory walls, hoping to frighten
the more timid boys. The dormitory was set on fire, and
all the boys' Sunday clothes, which were laid out on the
beds, were ruined. As might be expected, the phosphorus
left its mark on Algernon too, burning him quite badly.

On another occasion he put beeswax on the seat in
front of him in the school chapel, upsetting the service
and spoiling the boys' trousers.

Wilfred's father was a brilliant classic scholar, with a
gift for languages and a great interest in geology. He was
descended from the romantic and heroic Grenvilles of
Elizabethan days who sailed the Spanish Main and singed
the King of Spain's beard. No wonder that Tennyson's
ballad, *Revenge,* was one of Wilfred's favorite poems
as a boy, for it tells how Sir Richard Grenville fought
his small ship against fifty-three Spanish ships:

> "Shall we fight or shall we fly?
> Good Sir Richard, tell us now,
> For to fight is but to die!
> There'll be little of us left by the time this sun be set."
> And Sir Richard said again: "We be all good English
>   men.
> Let us bang these dogs of Seville, the children of the
>   devil,
> For I never turned my back upon Don or devil yet."
>
> Sir Richard spoke and he laughed, and we roared a
>   hurrah, and so

The little *Revenge* ran on sheer into the heart of
  the foe,
With her hundred fighters on deck, and her ninety
  sick below;
For half of their fleet to the right and half to the
  left were seen,
And the little *Revenge* ran on through the long sea-
  lane between. . . .
And the sun went down, and the stars came out far
  over the summer sea,
But never a moment ceased the fight of the one and
  the fifty-three. . . .

They were now in a desperate plight.
But Sir Richard cried in his English pride,
"We have fought such a fight for a day and a night
As may never be fought again!
We have won great glory, my men!
And a day less or more
At sea or ashore,
We die—does it matter when?
Sink me the ship, Master Gunner—sink her, split
  her in twain!
Fall into the hands of God, not into the hands of
  Spain!"

He was taken aboard one of the Spanish ships.

But he rose upon their decks, and he cried:
"I have fought for Queen and Faith like a valiant
  man and true;

I have only done my duty as a man is bound to do.
With a joyful spirit I Sir Richard Grenville die!"
And he fell upon their decks, and he died.

Wilfred's mother, who was born in India, came of a
family of distinguished soldiers, and she was able to tell
the boys many thrilling tales of their exploits.

From Parkgate, the estuary of the river Dee stretches
in sand-flats to the Welsh shore about five miles away.
At low tide the sandbanks and marshes are interlaced
with a network of channels and pools, which fill silently
and treacherously as the tide comes in. Many people have
been trapped and drowned in the deeper channels,
whirlpools, and quicksands of this deceptive river.

Charles Kingsley, who was related to the Grenfells,
visited them frequently. His poem *The Sands of Dee*
tells of one such tragedy:

> "O Mary, go and call the cattle home,
>   And call the cattle home,
>   And call the cattle home
>   Across the sands of Dee!"
> The western wind was wild and dank with foam,
>   And all alone went she.
>
> The western tide crept up along the sand,
>   And o'er and o'er the sand,
>   And round and round the sand,
>   As far as eye could see.

The rolling mist came down and hid the land:
    And never home came she.

"Oh! is it weed, or fish, or floating hair—
    A tress of golden hair,
    A drowned maiden's hair
   Above the nets at sea?
Was never salmon yet that shone so fair
    Among the stakes on Dee."

They rowed her in across the rolling foam,
    The cruel crawling foam,
    The cruel hungry foam,
   To her grave beside the sea:
But still the boatmen hear her call the cattle home
    Across the sands of Dee!

Wilfred, however, spent many happy days wandering over the sands, exploring the channels, shooting birds, fishing, and bathing. Sometimes he crossed over to the Welsh coast, and if the tide filled the channels he simply swam across them, and so he came to know the river intimately. Even the whirlpools held no fears for him: in his autobiography he describes how he used to plunge into one on the Cheshire side of the river and allow the swirling current to sweep him to the opposite bank.

Up the estuary, across the great salt-water marshes, was the Great Cop, an embankment intended to connect

England and Wales. The project was never completed, because no foundations could be made in the quicksands. Wilfred often stood on the end of the Cop where the workmen had abandoned their shovels and picks and trucks as though they had suddenly fled in a panic. To him it seemed like the banks of the Red Sea after the sea had closed in on Pharaoh and his hosts.

Occasionally the village fishermen would allow the boys to go with them in their boats when they fished overnight at the mouth of the Dee.

When the northwesterly gales came Wilfred would help the fishermen to make their boats fast, but sometimes the enormous waves would dash the boats against the sea-wall, or even lift them bodily over the wall on to the roadway. All these early adventurous days taught Wilfred many things about the sea and small boats that were to be very useful to him in later life.

During the school holidays Wilfred's father and mother often went abroad. The boys, left at home, had the run of the school buildings and grounds, and this probably gave them more enjoyment than if they had gone away themselves. Once, when their father and mother had left, they scraped together enough money to send a telegram to a favorite cousin in London, saying, "Dear Sid, come down and stay the holidays. Father has gone to Aix." To their dismay, a telegram in reply said,

"Not gone yet. Father." Their parents had stayed overnight at Cousin Sid's house. Fortunately they had enjoyed the joke, and Sid was allowed to come.

Wilfred and his brothers were expected to attend church every Sunday morning and evening during termtime, but on mornings only during holidays. The long sermons made these attendances very tedious, and Wilfred made all kinds of excuses to avoid going. He invented headaches and even made his nose bleed. Sometimes he managed to sleep during the long prayers. The Grenfell boys passed the time in church melting toffee and chocolate on the hot-water pipes, until some telltale silver paper gave them away and the churchwarden reported the matter to their father, who was very angry indeed with them.

On their way to church, clad in their Eton suits and top-hats, which they hated, the Grenfells always encountered Nonconformist boys going to their chapel. These boys often wore what Wilfred called "gorgeous apparel"; one of them once wore an especially brilliant waistcoat, which caused the Grenfells to invent the name "Specklebelly," which became their name for all Nonconformists.

The one event on Sunday which the brothers did enjoy was the hour before tea, when their mother read to them from various books. Wilfred wrote later: "We used to lie on the floor, or anywhere about. I can tell those stories now. I have lived those hours over again many times since."[1]

Wilfred's mother was one of the major influences in his life. "She was my ideal of goodness," he wrote; "her deeds never belied her words; we never knew her to act in anger or unjustly."

In order to teach them the value of money, Mr. Grenfell gave his children a small bank account, to which he added five pounds every birthday. This was known as "pony money" because the boys were saving up to buy a pony. They never managed to save enough, but there came a time when a pony was given to them. They grew very fond of her, and she was very patient with them; they often fell over her head or over her tail, but she always waited for them to remount. When they had learned to ride they had many exciting races across the sands, matching their pony against their cousin's horse.

But Wilfred's main interest was in boats, and, helped by the village carpenter, he and his brothers were allowed to spend their savings on building a boat of their own. They wanted a boat that would allow them to drift or paddle silently down the deep channels in the river, so that they could reach flocks of birds feeding on the banks. When the boat was finished they were much hurt to hear a cousin say, "It looks awfully like a coffin." They painted it red and called it *The Reptile*, and it served

[1] W. T. Grenfell, *What Life Means to Me*

them very well until it capsized, upsetting Wilfred and a friend with their guns into the half-frozen water of the river. They ran home dripping and anxious because one of the guns had been borrowed from Wilfred's uncle. Fortunately they managed to salvage the guns the next day.

Wilfred and Algernon were keen collectors and na- turalists. Wilfred learned from an old fisherman how to snare, skin, and stuff wild birds, and while he stuffed the birds and manufactured rock bases his brother made the glass-fronted cases in which they could be mounted and displayed.

Algernon also specialized in collecting birds' eggs, while Wilfred collected butterflies and moths. Later on, they added collections of seaweeds, shells, and flowers. These collections taught them a great deal because they always identified and labeled their specimens with me- ticulous care. Their collections formed the foundation of the museum which is still to be found at Mostyn House School.

Grown-up relatives occasionally visited the Grenfells, but only the ones with odd mannerisms made any impression on the boys. Wilfred well remembered one great-uncle, a distinguished professor at Oxford. He was the only man who was able to argue for any length of time with their father. One evening they were present in the drawing-room at one of these debates. Their great-

uncle, who was rather small, stout, and pink, always
walked up and down as he talked. He grew so absorbed
in his argument that when he found a sofa in his way
he stepped up on the seat, climbed over the back, and
went straight on talking without a pause.

2

◆-◆-◆-◆-◆-◆-◆-◆-◆-◆-◆-◆-◆-◆-◆-◆

Wilfred Goes to
Marlborough College

WHEN WILFRED WAS fourteen he was sent to Marlborough
College, a famous public school which housed about
six hundred boys. Because he had learned to be so self-
reliant, he was able to look after himself, and although
everything was so strange and new, he settled down
much sooner than most boys do when they go to a new
school.

During the first week he was challenged to fight by
a boy who had already spent a year at Marlborough.
Wilfred was victorious, and, as a direct result, he was
never again troubled by bullies. Partly because he was
such a ready fighter and partly because he had a large,
untidy mop of hair, he became known as "The Beast."

At first Wilfred had to do his prep in an enormous
room with three hundred other boys, but he did little
work, for he found his lessons very easy. When he had to

learn something off by heart, he preferred to write it down on paper and learn it at meal-times or in chapel.

During the first term, he won a scholarship, and was transferred to a room where he did his prep with only twenty-eight other students.

Meals were served to the boys in the Big Hall, but the food was very poor. The pupils therefore got together into "brewing companies" and provided their own breakfast and supper. To make certain that their money would last out, the members handed it, at the beginning of term, to a school official whom they called "The Slug." He gave out set amounts every Saturday night.

Fifth Form members found "brewing" easy because they had the right to place a kettle or saucepan on the classroom fire. Younger boys had to fight for the right to a space on the gas-stoves in the Big School.

As if this were not enough, Fourth Formers had, at times, to sit around the classroom while the Fifth Formers sat in the center, nonchalantly cooking and eating their suppers.

Wilfred seldom attended breakfast in the Big School, but, like all the other boys, he had to attend dinner and tea because absence was forbidden and lateness punished with fifty lines. He was often late, so kept a stock of lines which he had written out during school lessons. Occasionally, he even got other boys to write his lines for him.

Games were compulsory, and anyone who missed them was punished by the boys themselves, and this was considered a great disgrace. In order to encourage the pupils, there was an excellent system of classifying all the players. At the top came the first team, next came "the Forty," who wore velvet caps with tassels, then "the Sixty," who wore velvet caps with silver braid, then "the Eighty," and even "the Hundred." Boys could be transferred to the next grade, and were constantly striving to achieve this.

Afternoon games were taken very seriously, and when there was to be an important match, hungry boys were often, to their great disgust, ordered by the captains not to eat the "bollies," or suet puddings. This was all the more trying because noontime dinner was the only really solid meal of the day, and the bollies were particularly satisfying.

Beer, which the boys called "swipes," was served freely at dinner, and every one had as much as he liked. In addition, those boys who had house colors had swipes served to them at the end of every match.

The gates at the main entrance to the school were guarded by a lodge-keeper, and it was a serious offense to come in late. Wilfred once waited an hour outside the gates, hoping for a delivery van or cart to give him a lift. Fortunately, a parent coming to visit a boy in the sick-room arrived in a four-wheeled cab. Wilfred jumped on the step, and the person in the cab, realizing what was happening, kept the porter in conversation on the other side of the cab while Wilfred got clear.

There were, of course, strict rules preventing boys from going beyond certain boundries. Wilfred broke these rules in order to get extra swimming. The college had a good open-air swimming-pool on the river Kennet, and the boys were allowed one dip a day. If a boy was caught breaking this rule, he was suspended from swimming for a week, or even longer. But Wilfred soon discovered that the Sixth Formers in charge found it very difficult indeed to pick out offenders among the hundreds of boys in the water.

Of course, there were ways of getting in and out of the school grounds in spite of the high railings. A friend showed Wilfred how to get in by going a long way round and climbing over the laundry roof. He was very glad of this information on one occasion.

One of the older boys was much bolder. He wanted to get back into school, so he waited outside the railings until it was dusk, and then walked in through the masters' garden. He saw one of the instructors coming toward him, so he hurried forward and, imitating one of the other masters' voices, called out, "Night-night," and got away without being discovered.

Wilfred found the near-by Savernake Forest a wonderful place for adding to his collection of moths and

butterflies, and he often broke bounds with his butter-
fly net hidden under his coat. The best time to capture
moths was at night, and the thrill of being out of doors
on a beautiful summer evening while everyone else
was inside often made him dance for joy on the grass.
Using a dark lantern to help him to see, he would paint
the tree-trunks with a sweet, sticky, sugar concoction
which trapped the moths. Then he had the fascinating
task of visiting the trees, to see what specimens he had
captured.

Attendance at chapel was compulsory for all boys, and
lateness was punished by lines and the loss of a half-
holiday. At the entrance to the chapel were two iron
gates. A bell tolled for five minutes, then there was
silence for one minute, and then the bell tolled once
more. At that moment, the two masters who were holding the gates would close them, and the boys left outside
were late. Twice while Wilfred was at Marlborough,
panic-stricken boys rushed the gates at the last moment,
and the masters were unable to close them. In one case,
the boys were forgiven because the bell had been
sounded ten seconds too soon. In the other case, because
a master had been injured, a half-holiday was stopped.

Boys would run to the iron gates with shirts and col-
lars unbuttoned, shoes unlaced, and pulling on jackets
and waistcoats. They could usually be dressed by the
time they got to the chapel door. Inside the chapel,

masters checked to see who was absent. The only excuse
for absence was sickness, or scratched faces or knees,
caused by falling in the rush to reach the gates.

The old school doctor, whose nickname was "Fungi,"
and whom new boys often called "Dr. Fungi" by mistake, could be relied upon to help. But boys who pretended to be ill to get out of lessons or chapel usually
had to swallow a dose of very nasty medicine.

When he was sixteen, Wilfred developed a bad cough,
so he was sent off to the South of France for the winter.
He stayed with an aunt, and soon made friends with two
charming girls who lived in the same house. He had been
ordered to get out into the open air as much as possible,
and he and his new friends roamed over the hills, hunting for butterflies and moths. They kept frogs in boxes
equipped with little ponds and ladders for the frogs to
climb. They also kept trapdoor spiders, and spent much
time breeding butterflies and moths.

They had horses to ride and a beautiful beach at
which they could swim.

Wilfred and another boy were allowed to go to the
Carnival at Nice, where, disguised as a clown and a
clergyman, they had the time of their lives.

On Sundays, Wilfred went to the English Church, but
in later years all he could remember was the fact that the
clergyman had a peculiar way of saying all his "h's"
and "s's" as "sh," so he would say "shuman" for "hu-

man," and he always prayed that God would "shave the Queen."

Wilfred wrote home so enthusiastically about his holiday that his father wrote back saying that he had arranged for him to have lessons with a tutor so that he would not fall behind with his work.

During the following summer, Wilfred returned to Marlborough.

One of Wilfred's friends there was known as "Mad G." He was brilliant at mathematics and chemistry, and he and Wilfred spent many enjoyable hours talking over the problems they were set in these subjects. At night, Mad G. would often sit at the foot of Wilfred's bed and talk him to sleep, telling him about a new plan he had for a self-steering torpedo or a reliable flying-machine.

Mad G. was unpopular, however, because he hated games and the old customs that were followed rigidly by the other boys. He took no trouble with his appearance, and his hands were always stained by chemicals.

Although Mad G. did not complain, Wilfred found that he was being bullied by other boys, and he set out to protect him. This was no easy task, for not only did Wilfred have to see that he met the bullies in ones and twos, but some of his own friends resented the help he was giving Mad G.

One prize-day, Mad G.'s parents came to see their son

receive his prizes. Mad G.'s mother, who must have learned about Wilfred's friendship with her boy, met Wilfred in the quad and, to his horror, kissed him in front of all the other pupils.

Later, Wilfred spent many enjoyable holidays with Mad G. at his home in North Wales, where there was not only rough shooting, boating, rock-climbing, and swimming, but also the friendship of a delightful family.

3

❖—❖—❖—❖—❖—❖—❖—❖—❖—❖—❖—❖—❖—❖

Wilfred Decides to
Become a Doctor

WHEN WILFRED WAS eighteen years old, his father decided
to give up teaching and accepted the post of chaplain to
the London Hospital, in Whitechapel Road.

Mostyn House School was leased for seven years so
that when he was old enough, Algeron could take over
the headmastership.

Wilfred, who had never thought about it before, now
had to decide what his future career was going to be.
For a time he believed he would like to follow his uncles
as soldiers in India; then it was suggested that he should
become a missionary or a clergyman. But he decided
against these suggestions.

Then his father arranged for him to ask the advice of
their family physician. The doctor, who was a great
favorite with the Grenfell family, had a large country
practice, which he covered on horseback. He was a good

doctor and a good friend. He must have known all about the Grenfell boys' many pranks, played in the absence of their parents, but he never gave them away.

The only thing that Wilfred remembered in later years about his visit was the doctor taking down a large jar from which he produced a pickled human brain. Wilfred wrote in his autobiography, *A Labrador Doctor*:

"I was thrilled with entirely new emotions. That this weird, white, puckered-up mass could be the transmitter of all that made man, that it controlled our physical strength and growth and our responses to life, that it made one into Mad G., and another into me—why, it was absolutely marvelous."

Wilfred's mind was made up, and when his father suggested that he should either go to Oxford or join him at the London Hospital and University, to study medicine, Wilfred, without hesitation, chose London.

The London Hospital, which was the largest in Britain, was surrounded by the most appallingly squalid and crowded slums, where large numbers of people lived in abject poverty and misery, and where violence and crime were commonplace.

Although the hospital had nine hundred beds, these were always full, and extra beds had to be pushed in wherever there was space.

The practical experience gained by students in such a hospital was very wide and very useful, but Wilfred found that many of the lectures he was expected to attend were a complete waste of time. The students treated these lectures as a joke, and were so unruly that many of the lecturers could not get a hearing. Wilfred, for instance, attended only two botany lectures. At the first, someone spilled carbon bisulphide over the professor's platform, and the smell was so overpowering that the lecture had to be abandoned. At the second lecture, two pigeons were set free, and the students tried either to capture them or to stir them up with peashooters. The professor said, "Gentlemen, if you do not wish to learn, you are at liberty to leave," and the whole class walked out.

The chemistry professor was brilliant but very eccentric, and there was always pandemonium at his lectures. Sometimes, when he turned his head away from the students, he was pelted with peas and would leave the lecture theater in despair.

Most of the students fell into the habit of tipping the beadle, who automatically marked them as having attended the lectures.

Physiology and anatomy, however, were better taught, but it was only when Sir Frederick Treves became lecturer in anatomy and surgery that it was really worth while attending the lectures.

In spite of all this, Wilfred was able to pass the preliminary examination for Bachelor of Medicine.

As might be expected, he took an enthusiastic and very active interest in the athletic life of the University. He became secretary of the cricket, football and rowing clubs. He rowed in the inter-hospital races, played football, and threw the hammer. During the one term he was resident at Oxford, he gained his blue by playing in the University rugby team.

One night in 1885, when Wilfred was returning from visiting a patient in Shadwell, he stopped at a Moody and Sankey evangelistic meeting. He was much impressed with the way in which Moody conducted the meeting, and returned on another night, when Kynaston and C. T. Studd, the famous cricketers, spoke at a similar gathering. He decided there and then that, in the future, he would always do what he thought Christ would have done in his place as a doctor.

He began to teach a Sunday-school class, and, together with a young Australian student, he visited the sordid underground lodging-houses where the very poor were allowed to sleep for twopence a night. Here they held services and sang hymns. Sometimes they had to subdue drunken men before they could get a hearing.

He did not have much success with his Sunday-school classes until he began to teach boxing and physical training. This was carried out in the Grenfells' own dining-room, which was cleared every Saturday night, the furniture being pushed out through the window. These classes were very successful indeed.

Unfortunately, the clergyman in charge of the Sunday school could not accept this way of teaching, and Wilfred finally resigned from the school.

He joined his Australian friend in wrestling with a very difficult Sunday school for some wild, untamed London waifs. If the schoolroom was opened before the supervisors were there, it was liable to be wrecked and anything movable stolen. If boys were thrown out or locked out, they would climb up to the windows and defiantly wave the stolen goods. Several times Wilfred was pelted with stones and mud. There was constant war between the police and these waifs.

Wilfred finally gave up this school because his original Sunday-school pupils came and pleaded with him to continue his classes with them in his dining-room on Sundays.

In addition, he and his friend fought against drunkenness by visiting public houses and distributing leaflets. On one occasion, his friend was held by several men while whisky was poured down his throat, but when a similar attack was made on Wilfred, his athletic training proved too much for those who tried to hold him.

During the long summer vacations, Wilfred and his brother Algernon used to hire an old fishing-smack and sail in the Irish Sea. They began their voyages from

Anglesey, carrying fishing gear and a gun, and whenever
they needed fresh supplies of food, they simply landed
at one of the many small ports on the coast.

Algernon proved a wonderful cook, but the friends
the brothers took with them were quite unused to the
sea, and, as the navigational instruments were few and
unreliable, it was a wonder that they ever got anywhere.

They dressed in shorts and shirts, which was so unusual in those days that one lady asked Wilfred if he
was an Eskimo and offered him a job.

They had all kinds of adventures: once their boat
was nearly wrecked off the Isle of Man, while on another
occasion it was blown out to sea off Dynllyn, with no
one aboard. One night they ran into Ramsey Harbor
and tied up at the first bollard they could find in the
darkness. Then they went to sleep. They were awakened
next morning by the sound of water pouring onto the
deck. They rushed out to find that the tide had gone
out, leaving them high and dry on the mud, while a
large sewer was discharging its contents onto their
decks.

Fishing, swimming and shooting, with occasional expeditions ashore to visit castles or climb mountains,
gave them holidays they remembered all their lives.

When Wilfred returned to London and told his
Sunday-school pupils about these wonderful experiences,

it suddenly occurred to him that there was no reason why he should not share his holidays with them, so during the following summer he took thirteen boys to Anglesey. They had three tents, an old, deserted factory, and an uninhabited gorge by the sea to live in.

All the boys had to wear shorts and shirts, and everyone had to bathe before he got any breakfast.

They had an old lifeboat, which some of the boys took out each day, fishing and picnicking, but no boy was allowed in the boat until he could swim.

Climbing Snowdon became one of the favorite annual expeditions. It was carried out by land and by water. Half the boys walked overland to the Menai Straits, crossing by the Suspension Bridge. They spent the night at Trevorth, where they were splendidly fed and slept on beds of clean straw in the large stables. The other half of the boys came around the island by boat, anchoring on the south side of the Straits and joining the others at Trevorth. Then they all walked through Bethesda, climbed to the summit and returned to spend another night at Trevorth.

The number of boys taken increased to thirty in the second year and to nearly a hundred in later years.

The boys returned home with vivid memories of boating and fishing expeditions on rocky coasts; of scrambling up rough mountain paths; of campfire songs and stories; and of the comradeship of their friends.

Above all, they remembered the skill and daring of Wilfred as he sailed and swam and climbed. As one of them said many years later, "It was mainly by his own example that he brought the claims of Christ before us. It made me feel—well, if he is a Christian, I want to be one, too."

It is interesting that Wilfred was doing this work long before the first Boy Scout camps or school camps were organized.

After spending two years at the hospital and passing certain examinations, Wilfred Grenfell began "walking the hospitals," and spent a great deal of time with other students in following famous doctors and surgeons around the wards as they visited their patients.

His first task was to write down all the details of a certain number of patients, and he had to be ready to answer any questions about them when they were visited by the hospital doctors or visiting specialists.

Later, he became a "dresser," which meant that he had to take care of a number of patients who were waiting for an operation. The surgeons and doctors in charge made sure that their dressers did this job thoroughly and conscientiously.

During this time, great changes were taking place in the methods used by surgeons, and Wilfred's chief, Sir Frederick Treves, was one of the first men to insist on scrupulous cleanliness in the operating theater.

Wilfred saw many victims of criminal, murderous attacks, disfigured and maimed by people who were drunk, and from this time began his hatred of intoxicating drinks and the people who profited by their sale.

4

❖—❖—❖—❖—❖—❖—❖—❖—❖—❖—❖—❖—❖

Help for the North Sea
Fishermen

WILFRED SOMETIMES found North Sea fishermen among
the patients in the London Hospital. He discovered that
if the fishermen were injured at sea, there were no doctors to attend to them, and they could be brought ashore
only when the catches were being sent back to market.
Many fishermen died, and many went through great
suffering before reaching a hospital.

Each fishing-vessel was supposed to return home
every two or three months, and the men were entitled to
a day ashore for every week spent at sea. But in fact the
fishermen lived with the fishing fleet for months at a
time. The boats, which were quite small, stayed at sea
summer and winter. The shallow waters of the North
Sea, whipped up by fierce gales, made dangerous seas,
which constantly broke over the decks of the fishing-
boats with their low freeboard. Conditions were there-

fore very primitive, and the work was hard and dangerous. Grog ships, which sold alcohol and tobacco, moved
in and out of the fishing fleet and made large profits.

Sir Frederick Treves, who had recently made a trip
among the fishing-vessels, told Wilfred that a trawler
had been chartered by a small body of men interested
in the welfare of the deep-sea fishermen. This boat had
been sent out in order to hold simple religious services,
and so give the fishermen an alternative to spending
time on the grog vessels when fishing was slack. The
skipper was trained in ambulance work so that he could
give first aid to injured fishermen. But what they really
needed was a young doctor who would go out and not
only treat injuries, but also help with the religious
services.

Wilfred, who was now a qualified doctor, volunteered
to go out with the trawler.

He went to join his ship at Yarmouth on a dark night
in January, 1887. He was startled to find himself standing on the quayside, looking down at a tiny vessel only
a little larger than the old fishing-smack which he and
his brother used during their summer holidays. In the
darkness, he grabbed the rigging and began to slide
down in a series of jerks. Too late to save him came a
voice which shouted from below, "Mind the rigging!
It's just been tarred and greased."

He found the small ship to be spotlessly clean, with

a steward clad in a snow-white suit, and a crew of good-humored, independent, efficient seamen. He liked the look of them and felt that the voyage was going to be successful.

Wilfred was surprised to find that their first task was to sail to Ostend, to pick up four tons of tobacco, which, free from duty, could be sold to the fishermen at half the price charged by the grog ships.

It was so bitterly cold that the ship got frozen in at Ostend, and, in order to free themselves, they had to get a steamer to go around them, to smash the ice.

For the next two months they stayed at sea, and not once during the whole time was their deck free of ice and snow.

The fishing fleets carried over twenty thousand men and boys, whom Wilfred found to be cheerful, daring, brave and resourceful.

Each fleet had an "admiral" and a "vice-admiral," who would signal by flags or rockets to tell the other ships what to do.

Wilfred's trawler was expected to visit as many of the fleets as possible and arrange for a reliable ship in each fleet to take on a stock of tobacco. These ships flew blue bunting so that the other vessels would know them. They opened for business every morning, keeping as far to the leeward of the grog ship as possible, so that the men could not visit both. Nineteen of these depot ships were finally organized.

Wilfred was astonished to find that, apart from a sextant, the trawler carried no navigational instruments, and he was much puzzled to know how they could tell where they were. He found that the lead, which was used to find the depth of the sea, had a cup on the bottom filled with sticky grease. When the lead was hauled in, the sand, mud, or rock from the sea bottom was shown to the captain, and this told him where he was. This method of navigation had become second nature to the fishing fleet skippers, for they had served on such craft since boyhood.

The catches were rowed in small boats to fast cutters, which rushed the fish to market. This was undoubtedly the most dangerous part of the fishermen's work. To launch a small boat in half a gale and fill her up with heavy boxes of fish was bad enough, but then came the task of rowing over to the cutter in mountainous seas and the almost superhuman task of getting the boxes on to the cutter. As many as twenty or thirty boats would be tied up alongside the cutter, and it was not unusual for her rail to roll under the water and come up again under the keels of some of the small boats, tipping them upside-down. The men in the boats would be thrown into the sea and knocked to pieces among the madly tossing craft.

Because less fish reached the market when the weather was bad, it brought the best prices then, so skippers and some of the daredevils among their crews were always eager to row fish over on even the worst days. Many men

were killed in this fashion, until the Board of Trade
made a ruling that a captain could be charged with
manslaughter if any of his crew were drowned while
boarding fish.

In the early days, the ships' boys, who were appren-
ticed to the fishery masters, came, for the most part, from
industrial and reformatory schools and had no relations
to look after them. This system seems to have worked
better than could be expected, and it certainly produced some excellent seamen. But occasionally the system was abused. The apprentices were not entitled to
wages, but received pocket-money only, and it could
happen that a whole ship's crew, being under twenty-
one years of age, would be apprentices.

There were no seamen's unions, and sometimes the
apprentices were treated very cruelly by the skippers,
who were responsible for discipline in their ships and
who had themselves been brought up in a rough school.

The captains sometimes devised their own punish-
ments for their ships' boys. One lad who had been re-
peatedly careless in cooking the duff for dinner was forced
to take the cinders from the galley fire, go to the forward
rigging, take one cinder at a time, climb the rigging to
the crosstrees, throw the cinder into the sea, come down
the opposite rigging, and repeat the act until all the
cinders had gone.

Another boy, who had left the cabin untidy, was

forced, instead of going to bed, to draw up a bucketful of sea water and empty it, with a teaspoon, into another bucket . . . and continue to do so until morning.

Not only did Wilfred tend the sick, hold well-attended religious services and distribute comforts, but he made many friends. He wrote later in *A Labrador Doctor*:

"One soon became so friendly with the men that one would not return at night to the ship, but would visit around and rejoin the Mission ship boarding fish the next day, to see patients coming for aid. Though it was strictly against sea rules for skippers to be off their vessels all night, that was a rule, like all others on the North Sea, as often marked in the breach as in the observance. A goodly company would get together yarning and often singing and playing games until it was time to haul the trawl and light enough to find their own vessels and signal for boats."

Wilfred loved fun and adventure, and he had a very keen sense of humor. Some of the old fishermen who knew him in his early days on the North Sea remembered him more for this than for anything else. One old sailor who remembered him very well said, "He was a perfect young divil for fun."

In order to pay its way, the Mission ship fished like the other vessels, so Wilfred would often have to turn out in all kinds of weather and at all times, to help with hauling the nets or to give a hand with the many other dangerous and strenuous jobs of the ordinary fisherman.

Grenfell's work was so successful that more Mission ships joined the fleet, and the work was extended to the herring fleets in the Irish Sea and the seas west of Ireland.

Besides helping the fishermen, Grenfell and his friends landed to attend to farmers living in isolated places and lighthouse-keepers. To reach the latter in rough seas, they sometimes caught a line from an overhanging crane and were swung up and around into a trapdoor in the side of the lighthouse. To get back into the boat, they had to dangle from the crane until they were grabbed by the waiting men in the boat below.

As time went on, the grog ships were banished, and the sale of alcohol to fishermen at sea was banned by law.

By 1897, the Mission of Deep Sea Fishermen had a fleet of thirteen boats and several buildings ashore. Holland and France were now sending out hospital schooners as well. Not only were the grog ships banished, but the fishermen's conditions were greatly improved; moreover, many of the drinking-saloons frequented by fishermen were closed through lack of custom. In addition, little chapels where fishermen could worship were built in many places.

5

❖–❖–❖–❖–❖–❖–❖–❖–❖–❖–❖–❖–❖

Grenfell's First Visit to Labrador

In 1891, the Mission to Deep Sea Fishermen decided that medical help and supplies of comforts must be sent to the thousands of fishermen who worked along the inhospitable coasts of Labrador.

This meant that a small hospital ship would have to be equipped and sent across the Atlantic Ocean.

Dr. Grenfell, who was now twenty-six years old, was asked to attend a special meeting of the Council of the Mission. He was told about all the dangers and difficulties of such a trip, but when he was asked to take charge, he consented without hesitation.

He later discounted all lofty motives for his decision, saying that an adventure like sailing to Labrador, with all its exciting preparations, was just the kind of thing that appealed to his kind of mind and temperament.

He chose the *Albert*, a vessel of less than one hundred tons. He had her sails altered and her planking strengthened to withstand the pressure of the sea ice. A small

hospital was fitted out amidships, with bunks, an oper-
ating-table, surgical equipment and a dispensary.

As neither Grenfell nor his first mate had crossed the
Atlantic before, a Cornish skipper, Captain Trevize, was
engaged.

They sailed on June 15, 1892, from Yarmouth, but
contrary winds delayed them. On the twelfth day out,
they saw their first iceberg and narrowly avoided col-
liding with it in dense fog. On the seventeenth day, as
the fog lifted, they saw a high coastline crowded with
evergreens. They had made a landfall within a mile of
St. John's Harbour, their intended destination.

When they entered St. John's Harbour, they found
that, for the third time in its history, St. John's was in
flames. They counted thirteen enormous fires, while
smoldering ruins burst into flames again as the wind
fanned the embers into life. Only the brick chimney-
stacks remained standing.

In spite of all this destruction, the people were amaz-
ingly cheerful and uncomplaining, and found time to
show great interest in the expedition's plans. Of the
quarter of a million people living along the coasts of
Newfoundland and Labrador, nearly two hundred
thousand were engaged in the fishing industry, so any
scheme for improving the conditions of the fishermen
was bound to be warmly welcomed.

Dr. Grenfell had imagined that he would find a fishing

fleet like that in the North Sea, but, because of the fogs, each vessel worked independently and returned to port with its own catch. It was decided, therefore, to follow the fleet of about a thousand schooners which had just sailed north to the summer fishing-grounds, carrying thirty thousand fishermen, women and children.

This meant a voyage of some four hundred miles. The first four days of the journey passed in dense fog, which lifted only for a short time as they went by Cape Bauld, at the northeast corner of Newfoundland and felt their way blindly across the Straits of Belle Isle, to run parallel with the Labrador coast.

Then the fog suddenly lifted, and through all his years in Labrador, Dr. Grenfell never forgot this first exciting view. He wrote in *A Labrador Doctor*:

"Forty years have passed away since that day, and a thousand more important affairs which have occurred in the meantime have faded from my memory; but still its events stand out clear and sharp. Round Hill Island, covered with green verdure, so wonderful a landmark from the sea, its peaks capped with the fleecy mist of early morning, rose in a setting of the purest azure blue. For the first time I saw its ruddy cliffs, their ledges picked out with the homes of myriads of birds. Its feet were bathed in the dark, rich green of the Atlantic waters, edged by the line of white breakers, where the gigantic swell lazily hurled immeasurable mountains of

water against its titanic bastions, evoking peals of sound
like thunder from its cavernous recesses—a very riot
of magnificence. It answers to the description of St.
John's Island given by John Cabot as his first sight of
the American continent. The great schools of whales,
noisily slapping the calm surface of the sea with their
huge tails as in an abandon of joy, dived and rose, and
at times threw the whole of their mighty carcasses right
out of the water for a bath in the glorious morning sunshine. The shoals of fish everywhere breaching the water,
and the silver streaks which flashed beneath our bows
as we lazed along, suggested that the whole vast ocean
was too small to hold its riches.

"When we realized that practically no man had ever
lived there, and few had ever seen it, it seemed to over-
whelm us, coming as we did from the crowded island
of our birth, where notices not to trespass haunted the
dreams of the average man.

"A serried rank of range upon range of hills, reaching
north and south as far as the eye could see from the
masthead, was rising above our horizon behind a very
surfeit of islands, bewildering the minds of men ac-
customed to our English and North Sea coastlines."

They finally found the fleet of schooners in a natural
harbor called Domino Run. There were greetings from
every side, and their ship was soon surrounded by small
boats from the schooners, crowded with curious fishermen inquiring who they were.

At once there were calls for the doctor, and these lasted until well on into the evening. It was only then that Dr. Grenfell, as he leaned over the ship's side to rest, noticed a poorly dressed man in a wretched little boat that hardly held together. The man hesitated . . . and finally told the doctor that he had no money to pay him, but there was a very sick man ashore. Would he come and see what he could do for him?

Grenfell followed the man to a small hut covered with sods. The floor was made with pebbles from the beach, and the earth walls were damp and chilly. Wooden bunks were built around the walls. Six poorly clad children were huddled in one corner, while on one of the lower bunks a very sick man lay coughing, as a thin, shabbily dressed woman gave him sips of cold water from a spoon. A small stove was the only furniture.

The man was extremely ill, and could have been saved only by careful nursing in a hospital. Dr. Grenfell did what he could, but when he called back to see the family in two months' time the man was dead and buried, and the wife and children were destitute.

Dr. Grenfell treated about nine hundred patients on this trip and saw much misery and pain that could have been avoided if a doctor had been within reach.

There was no education for the children, and there were no social services that could have improved living conditions. In spite of all this, the fishermen were cheerful, generous, resourceful and uncomplaining.

This was a voyage very much after Grenfell's own heart, and, as he wrote later in *A Labrador Doctor*:

"We greatly enjoyed the adventure *qua* adventure. Mysterious fjords which wound out of sight into the fastnesses of unknown mountains, and which were entirely uncharted, fairly shouted an invitation to enter and discover what was round the next corner. Islands by the hundred, hitherto never placed on any map, challenged one's hydrographic skill. Families of strange birds, which came swinging seaward as the season advanced, suggested a virgin field for hunting. Berries and flowering plants, as excellent as they were unfamiliar, appealed for exploration. Great boulders perched on perilous peaks, torn and twisted strata, with here and there raised beaches and great outcrops of black traprock piercing through red granite cliffs in giant vertical seams—all piqued one's curiosity to know the geological story of this unknown land. Some stone arrow-heads and knives, brought to me by a fisherman, together with the memories that the Norse Vikings and their competitors on the scroll of discovery who made their first landfall on this the nearest section of the American coast to Europe, excited one's curiosity to know more of these shores. The dense growth of the evergreen trees abounding in every river valley and the exquisite streams with trout and salmon and seals attracted one whose familiarity with sport and forests was inseparably connected with notices to trespassers, and flatly contradicted the impression left by the predatory explorers of Columbus' age."

In October, the coming of the ice drove Dr. Grenfell and his crew south, and they put in at St. John's, to tell of their experiences and ask for help to solve the problems they had discovered on the coast. But the returning fishermen had already brought news of the doctor who had relieved great suffering and who had shirked no dangers to reach patients. So they found themselves very much in the news.

Meetings were held at which Grenfell told the story of his voyage. Gifts of money were promised, and a merchant offered a house which could be used as a hospital at Battle Harbour. One young man was so inspired by Grenfell's example that he decided to become a doctor and join the Mission. Nine years later, he became a member of the medical staff at Battle Harbour.

Grenfell and his crew set sail for home in splendid spirits. The voyage was uneventful—except that Grenfell was nearly left behind in mid-Atlantic! He wrote later:

"While playing cricket on deck, our last ball went over the side, and I after it, shouting to the helmsman to tack back. This he did, but I failed to cut him off the first time, as he got a bit rattled. However, we rescued the ball."

Back in England, Grenfell's report persuaded the Mission to go ahead with its work in Labrador, and at meetings in various parts of the country he aroused great interest and obtained many promises of money and support.

6

❖◆❖◆❖◆❖◆❖◆❖◆❖◆❖

The Second Year in Labrador

IN THE SPRING of 1893, Grenfell, after an enormous amount of preparatory work, sailed again for Labrador.

The *Albert* was re-equipped, and instructions were sent for converting the Battle Harbour house into a hospital with sixteen beds. In addition, a firm of Newfoundland merchants had presented a second hospital, which was to be shipped in sections and erected at Indian Harbour, two hundred miles north of Battle Harbour.

Two nurses and two doctors volunteered to travel from England and work in these new hospitals.

There was a real need for a steam-launch which could accompany the *Albert* and tow her in the narrow channels and inlets where her sails were useless. There was difficulty over raising enough money to buy such a vessel, but at last a tiny steam-launch, eight feet wide and forty-five feet long, was found lying up on the Chester racecourse. This launch was taken by canal to the river Mersey and hoisted aboard a liner and carried direct to St. John's.

The little ship was named the *Princess May,* and Grenfell prepared her for her voyage north. The Labrador sailors and fishermen didn't think much of the chances of the *Prinesss May* in their rough seas. Besides being so small, she was at least six years old, and because there was no coal available, she had to burn wood in her small firebox. This meant that the crew were chopping up wood endlessly.

Grenfell later confessed that he also had doubts about how the launch would behave, for he had had no time to give her a trial run. Her narrow beam was bound to make her roll severely in the Atlantic seas.

The *Albert* sailed north on May 6, and the *Princess May* followed the next day, carrying Grenfell with a cook-engineer. The *Princess May's* adventurous career began at once, when, after an hour afloat, the engineer called out to say that they had sprung a leak. Grenfell, however, managed to remedy this by driving home a strong wooden plug.

A dense fog now enveloped them, and, although they proceeded cautiously, they suddenly found themselves heading straight for a great cliff. Their compass was faulty.

They managed to reach Catalina Harbour safely, but next day, in a rough sea, they lost some of their deck gear.

They had many other adventures, but on the seventh day they crossed the Straits of Belle Isle and dropped anchor alongside the *Albert,* in Battle Harbour.

Here Grenfell found every one working extremely hard to get the hospital ready for its patients. After giving as much help as possible, the two Mission ships left. The *Albert* sailed north, carrying Dr. Curwen and Sister Williams, who were to work in the hospital at Indian Harbour. Dr. Bobardt, a young Australian, and Sister Carwardine were left to run the hospital at Battle Harbour.

The *Princess May* sailed south-west about one hundred miles from the entrance of the Straits of Belle Isle, visiting all the stations and giving much-needed medical and surgical help to the settlers.

Sailing back to Battle Harbour, the *Princess May* had several narrow escapes from disaster: once she ran aground on a flat-topped rock within a few yards of perpendicular cliffs; another time, the propeller refused to work, and the crew had to erect a sail. Fortunately, they met a sealing-steamer which was able to lend an engineer, who put things right for them.

They arrived back at Battle Harbour at the end of July, in time to see the first patients being put into comfortable beds in the hospital.

Two days later, the *Princess May* steamed north for Indian Harbour. Calls were made wherever a doctor was needed, and there were many unusual incidents.

One night as the *Princess May* lay hove to in dense fog, Grenfell heard stealthy footsteps on deck. A half-breed Eskimo came to the cabin door and asked for help for his daughter, who was lying seriously ill ashore. The doctor was soon being rowed through the darkness in the Eskimo's boat. On landing, they stumbled over broken rock for about a quarter of a mile, until they reached a small, overcrowded cottage. Grenfell found that his patient was too ill to be moved to the hospital and operated on the spot. It was not until some months later that he learned that the operation had saved the woman's life.

When the *Princess May* ran into Indian Harbour, they found, to their disappointment, that work had been held up on the new hospital by bad weather. Four weeks of wind and storm had prevented the landing of the sections.

It was decided that the *Albert* should stay near Indian Harbour and serve as a base for as much of the work of the hospital as was possible.

The *Princess May* again sailed north, revisiting Hopedale and the main stations of the Moravian Brethren, who had been working among the Eskimos of Labrador for a hundred and fifty years.

The Brethren had taught the natives to read and write in the Eskimo tongue, but translating the Bible had proved very difficult because many things had no

Eskimo names. For instance, no Eskimo had ever seen a sheep or a lamb, so, in the translating of the words "Lamb of God," the words "white seal" were used. Grenfell once explained this while speaking to an English audience. Months later, while unpacking clothing which had been sent out from England, he found a very crushed, dirty and dejected-looking toy lamb with a label round its neck saying, "Sent in order that the heathen may know better."

Grenfell found the Eskimos to be optimisic, good-natured and contented. They loved music, and their ability to do part playing and part singing impressed the doctor, who spent many enjoyable evenings listening to their brass bands and their Easter and Christmas carols. The doctor and his friends made records of the Eskimos singing, and these gave great joy when they were played back to them.

The magic lantern was very popular indeed with the Eskimos, and when lantern slides made from photographs of themselves were shown they were much intrigued and got up to feel themselves on the screen. On one occasion, when a picture was shown of an old Eskimo woman who had died during the winter, there was a great commotion. The Moravian Brethren explained that the Eskimos believed that her spirit had taken visible form and was revisiting them.

From Hopedale, the *Princess May* sailed north to visit

the other Moravian Mission stations. Because there were no charts, the Grenfell party took one of the Moravian Missionaries with them as a guide and interpreter. As Grenfell wrote later in *A Labrador Doctor*:

". . . one of the Brethren, Mr. Christopher Schmidt, joined the *Princess May* to help me find their northern stations among the plethora of islands which fringed the coast in that vicinity. Never in my life had I expected any journey half so wonderful. We travelled through endless calm fjords, runs, tickles, bays, and straits without ever seeing the open sea, and with hardly a ripple on the surface of the water. We passed high mountains and lofty cliffs, crossed the mouths of large rivers, left groves of spruce and fir and larches on both sides of us, and saw endless birds, among them the Canada goose, eider duck, surf scoters, and many commoner sea fowl. As it was both impossible and dangerous to proceed after dark, when no longer able to run we would go ashore and gather specimens of the abundant and beautiful sub-Arctic flora, and occasionally capture a bird or a dish of trout to help out our meagre larder."

They reached Okkak, the most northerly of the Eskimo stations, in late autumn. Then, because winter was approaching and there was a real danger of being marooned, they steamed southward at top speed.

At Hopedale, they found the *Albert* and about a hundred fishing-schooners that had gathered under the threat of the coming winter, before the final dash south. That Sunday, the Moravian chapel, which held four hundred people, was too small for the congregation which flocked to hear Dr. Grenfell's services, so Captain Trevize held an extra service in the *Albert*.

It was now clear that if the Mission workers were to race the winter and get safely to St. John's before the ice closed in, they would have to sail at once. There was, therefore, great anxiety when the *Princess May* was driven on to a rock; she was refloated and beached in Hopedale Harbour at low tide. Fortunately, the hull was still sound, although part of the keel had been torn away and some of the copper sheeting stripped. The propeller shaft was also badly bent. The crew did what repairs they could and decided to risk the journey south.

The *Albert* too had scraped heavily on the rocks, and the keel was damaged, but those aboard also decided to risk sailing.

The two vessels met very rough weather and had difficult and dangerous passages, but arrived safely at Battle Harbour on October 19.

They sailed from Battle Harbour in even worse weather. The *Albert* lost her boom and some of her canvas, but arrived safely at St. John's. But the *Princess May* became overdue, and rumors reached England that she had been lost with all hands. This seemed to be confirmed when a fishing-schooner sailed into St. John's with a broken flagstaff from which hung the doctor's blue flag.

The mail-steamer which was due to sail northward was asked to keep a sharp lookout. Near Cape St. John, they found the *Princess May* calmly taking on coal in a quiet cove. Captain Taylor, of the mail-steamer, was so relieved to see Grenfell that he flung his arms around him and hugged him.

Grenfell explained that they had lost their compass and flag in the heavy seas and that, running short of fuel, they had had to burn the top of the cabin. But he had not thought for a moment that anyone would be anxious about their safety.

Grenfell finally sailed into St. John's on November 10, after a voyage of over six hundred miles. He had treated over two thousand patients and had prevented many families from dying from want of food and clothing.

One of the problems of the poorer settlers was the "truck system." When they had furs or fish to sell, they took them to a trader, who paid them in food and other goods. They were never given money, and this nearly always meant that they were finally in debt to the trader.

On one occasion when the *Princess May* broke down, Dr. Grenfell went on ahead in the jolly-boat to visit a very poor family whose child had been taken to the hospital. When the steamer did not come, he had to

Top: Mostyn House School is the large building on the right. The sea-wall and mud-flat are in the foreground. *(From Wilfred Grenfell's Album, lent by D. Grenfell, Esq.) Bottom:* Grenfell with his brothers, Algernon and Cecil, in 1890, when Wilfred was a doctor on a mission ship in the North Sea.

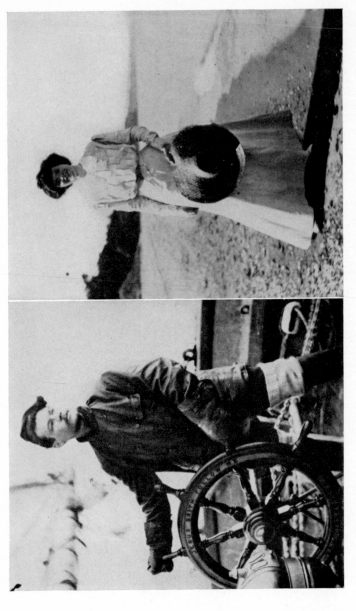

Left: Grenfell at the wheel in 1892. *Right:* "The girl in black" before her marriage to Grenfell.
(Photographs from Wilfred Grenfell's Album, lent by D. Grenfell, Esq.)

Grenfell with his dogs in the early days

Top: Interior of the original Battle Harbour Hospital. *Bottom:* Tea-time at the St. Anthony Orphanage.

Top: Grenfell in an Eskimo kayak. *(Photo H. T. Edwards)*
Bottom: The hospital ship *Maravel* surrounded by ice during a
summer medical cruise.

Top: The *Princess May*, 1893. *(From Wilfred Grenfell's Album, lent by D. Grenfell, Esq.) Bottom:* The S. S. *Strathcona II.*

Top: A Grenfell doctor off on a medical trip. *Bottom:* Modern transportation is now used. A nurse returning by helicopter to Hamilton Village from North-West River.

Top: Rear Admiral Donald MacMillan, who accompanied Peary on his North Pole explorations, and who led an expedition in Labrador, is showing Grenfell edible mushrooms. *Bottom:* As a magistrate, Dr. Grenfell often tried cases aboard his hospital ship.

(Photo Professor F. C. Sears)

Dr. Grenfell with a small patient who was badly burned

Sir Wilfred Grenfell at the wheel in later years

St. Anthony in winter

Battle Harbour: fish flakes laid out

Dr. Grenfell being greeted by the natives of Double Island

A Grenfell doctor and nurse landing at a small settlement to visit patients. *(Photo Chris Lund)*

Dr. Grenfell holding an Eskimo child patient. *(Photograph by Fred C. Sears, Amherst, Mass.)*

Sir Wilfred Grenfell's last visit to the coast in 1939

sleep in the tiny, one-roomed hut with the family. Five of the children huddled together in one bed and the parents and the rest of the family in the other bed. Dr. Grenfell slept on the floor in his sleeping-bag, with his nose close to a crack under the door so that he could get a breath of fresh air.

The window was sealed, for there was not a single blanket in the hut. When Grenfell asked what had happened to the blankets he had left the previous year, he was shown the trousers and coats that had been made from them.

In the morning, the visitor and the two eldest boys went out on a seal-hunt. In spite of their thin clothes, the boys did not seem to feel the cold.

Dr. Grenfell later sent the family some animal traps, and the following summer, when he called, they presented him with a fine silver-fox fur. He sold it and took back a load of goods for them. He helped this family several times in the same way, and they were never again in such want.

Experiences like this caused Dr. Grenfell in later years to establish stores at which poor people could trade, and he did this well knowing what opposition he would arouse among the traders.

7

The People of Labrador

LABRADOR forms the northeasterly coastal strip of Canada. It stretches eleven hundred miles north from the estuary of the St. Lawrence River, and is seven hundred miles across at its widest point.

When Grenfell first visited Labrador no one seemed to know who owned the country, and no one seemed to care very much. England, America, Canada, Newfoundland and France had all controlled parts of it at various times, but as the country began to be opened up and boundaries had to be defined, Canada and Newfoundland emerged as the countries mainly interested. The interior became part of the Canadian Province of Quebec, while Newfoundland administered the coastline. (Since 1949 Newfoundland has been incorporated with Canada.)

The coast of Labrador is rocky and forbidding, with innumerable islands and rocky inlets, making navigation very difficult.

Great storms sweep this coast, and dense fogs are common. Icebergs float about freely, and the sea becomes frozen in the winter months.

Newfoundland and Labrador are in the same latitude as England and Scotland. Battle Harbour, in the extreme south of Labrador, is almost on a parallel with London, and is the nearest point of North America to the Irish coast, being almost exactly halfway between New York and England. Labrador and Newfoundland, therefore, have the same length of day and night as England and Scotland. The difference in climate comes from the Gulf Stream, which warms the English coast, while Labrador is washed by the icy waters of the polar current.

The interior of Labrador forms an enormous plateau, much of it rocky and unfertile. It is known, however, that rich mineral deposits lie there. Moreover, forests of spruce, birch and aspen form great reserves which could be used for wood-pulp. The tremendous waterfalls are also a potential source of unlimited hydro-electric power.

Animals like the beaver, fox, lynx, marten, mink, otter, caribou deer and bear are found, and are hunted and trapped for their fur and skin.

Obviously, not many people could be expected to live in such a country. The original native inhabitants of Labrador were Eskimos and Indians. Montagnais Indians still roam in the interior. They are the descendants of the Algonquins who used to make war on the Eskimos.

As white settlers from Europe came into the country, the Eskimos retired north. Epidemics, which seemed to follow contact with white men, killed off many of them, so that now there are very few left.

Grenfell was much interested in the Eskimos and grew quite fond of them. He wrote the following description of them in *The Griffin,* the magazine of Mostyn House School:

"The Eskimo are a small-sized people, but some of them attain the height of five feet eight inches. They have flat features of an olive and not displeasing hue, jet black eyes and straight black hair. The men cut their hair straight across the forehead in a sort of 'Piccadilly' fringe, the remainder being allowed to grow down to the shoulders. Their dress consists of an upper garment of skin called a 'kossack.' This is in one piece, and is drawn up over the head in a sort of cowl. The nether limbs are encased in skin. Skin boots, which cover the leg as far as the knee, and possess very heavy soles, complete the costume.

"The Eskimo women carry their infants in the 'cowl,' which by the men is used as a head-covering. It is suspended over their backs, and there the infant rests quite cosily. At the back the women's garment runs almost down to the heel in a sort of tail, giving the wearer a grotesque appearance. When viewed from the side, the

Eskimo dress is most ludicrous in aspect. Considerable ingenuity is shown in the manufacture of these garments. The tendons from the reindeer serve them as thread, and with the aid of needles passed through fire and bent in the requisite way, they sew the skins together. The sole of the boot is very thick. It is rendered soft and pliable by being chewed. . . .

"The Eskimo are a merry, happy race of people, and very affectionate in their disposition. They endure pain with considerable fortitude. I have performed a number of surgical operations upon Eskimo, and when I have not given an anaesthetic the endurance shown was such that one would almost imagine it was an inanimate object and not a human being that was under the knife. They are very grateful for any service you may render them. . . .

"There are about 3000 Eskimo in that part of Labrador which I am familiar with. They live by catching seals and whales, and eating the blubber, using the skins for the purposes of clothing themselves. They hunt in their light 'kayaks,' or canoes. When seated in these a piece of skin is drawn from the edge of the place wherein they sit right up under their arms, preventing any water from entering, and rendering the buoyant little craft watertight. The method of catching the seals or whales is by harpooning them.

"The harpoon is ingeniously made of walrus tusk,

attached by a strip of hide to the end of a pole. To this is attached a buoy, made out of an inflated skin. When the harpoon is thrown the whale dashes away, but the appearance of the buoy indicates its locality. The Eskimo follows in his kayak, secures his prey and tows it ashore. . . . The Eskimo carry their wives with them, either sitting or lying on the stern of the kayak, from the mainland to the adjacent islands. This is done because the kayak will hold only one person. They are very liable to be upset. . . .

"The Eskimo play a kind of leap-frog in the water with the boats. Swiftly propelling their kayaks, which possess high pointed bows, the more active ride over their less skilful companions, forcing them down into the water. The only other game I have seen them play is hitting with sticks a kind of ball made out of an inflated skin."

The white settlers on the coast, who were few in number, were often very poor, and lived by catching fish in the summer and trapping fur animals in the winter. In addition to these people were the Labradormen, the Newfoundland fishermen who, with their families aboard, sailed up the coast between June and October for the summer fishing. The families either lived on board the fishing vessels or in huts built on the shore.

The people whom Dr. Grenfell went out to help were mainly the white fishermen and their families who, in a body about twenty thousand strong, visited the coast of Labrador every summer. It was later that he included the settlers of the Labrador and Newfoundland coast.

Some families were prosperous, but many were extremely poor and often found themselves on the verge of starvation.

As Grenfell wrote in *A Labrador Doctor*:

"The privations which the inhabitants of the French or Treaty shore and of Labrador have had to undergo, and their isolation from so many of the benefits of civilization, have had varying effects on the residents of the Coast. The Labrador fishermen of today find their counterpart in the people of the Southern mountains of the United States. They speak the same Elizabethan English, overlaid, to be sure, with a vernacular of the sea. They were caught behind the Arctic waters of the North, an eddy of civilization, just as the Southern mountaineers were cut off by their hilly fastnesses from the onward march of what we so glibly style 'progress.' They are reactionary in matters of religion and education; and their very 'speech betrays them,' belonging, as do so many of their expressions, to the days when the Pilgrims went up to Canterbury, or when a certain tinker wrote of another and more distant pilgrimage to the City of Zion.

"The people are, naturally, Christians of a devout and simple faith. Their superstitions are of the date and brand when witches and hobgoblins and charms and amulets were generally accepted beliefs. But they are not very different from some which we at times find that we do not altogether discredit. Let's touch wood, shall we?"

One man's charm against sea-boils was to cut his nails on Monday and burn the parings. Most of the people carried charms written on bits of paper which were sewn up in little bags to be worn around the neck.

Dr. Grenfell found one man who wore around his neck a piece of string from which hung a large haddock's fin-bone. This was a charm against rheumatism. To be effective, the fish's fin had to be cut out before the fish, after being taken from the water, touched anything.

One day the doctor and his friends were surprised to see a family moving from their home in the middle of the fishing season. This family believed that a spirit had taken possession of their house during the night, so they were moving to another place during the day, while the spirit was asleep.

A fox's or wolf's head was often suspended from the ceiling, and this was supposed to twist away from the direction of the wind.

One of Grenfell's colleagues once visited a village forty miles south of St. Anthony, to find that all the men were out on the ice, killing a number of seals that had come in. Unfortunately, many of the men had been attacked by snow-blindness and could not benefit from their good fortune. The doctor spent a busy night treating these men. Next morning, he was astonished to see that his patients had used his prescription on one eye only. The other eye had been treated with tansy poultices and sugar, which were the local remedies. The men thought it too risky to trust entirely to the newfangled doctoring.

Traveling along the coast at this time was very difficult. The little coastal steamers were so crowded that people could not hope to sleep, and often had hardly enough room even to sit down. All the goods and luggage had to be transferred to small boats. In *A Labrador Doctor*, Grenfell describes a typical landing of such goods:

"The hatch of the steamer is opened, a most unmusical winch commences operations—and a sewing machine emerges *de profundis*. This is swung giddily out over the sea by the crane and dropped on the thwarts of a waiting punt. One shudders to think of the probably fatal shock received by the vertebrae of the machine. One's sympathies, however, are almost immediately enlisted in the interest and fortunes of a young and voiceful pig, which, poised in the blue, unwillingly experiences for the moment the fate of the coffin of the Prophet. Great shouting ensues as a baby is carried down the ship's ladder and deposited in the rocking boat. A bag of beans, of the variety known as haricot, is the next candidate. A small hole has been torn in a corner of a burlap sack, out of which trickles a white and ominous stream.

The last article to join the galaxy is a tub of butter. By a slight mischance, the tub has 'burst abroad,' and the butter, a golden and gleaming mass, with unexpected consideration, having escaped the ministrations of the winch, is passed from one pair of fishy hands to another, till it finds a resting-place by the side of the now quiescent pig."

Although the people were very poor and suffered from many diseases brought about by their poverty, they were unfailingly hospitable and generous. They would turn out of their beds at any time to make a stranger comfortable, and they would share whatever food they had, never expecting or asking for payment. In his notebook of 1895, Dr. Grenfell wrote:

"The desolation of Labrador at this time is easy to understand. No Newfoundlanders are left north of us; not a vessel in sight anywhere. The ground is all under snow, and everything caught over with ice except the sea. I must describe one house, for it seems a marvel that any man could live in it all winter, much less women and children. It is ten feet by twenty, one story high, made of mud and boards, with half a partition to divide bedroom from sitting-room kitchen. If one adds a small porch filled with dirty, half-starved dogs and refuse of every kind, an ancient and dilapidated stove in the sitting part of the house, two wooden benches against the walls, and two boarded-up beds, one has a fairly accurate description of the furnishings. Inside are fourteen persons, sleeping there, at any rate for a night or two. The ordinary regular family of a man and wife and four girls is to be increased this winter by the man's brother, his wife, and four boys from twelve months to seven years of age. His brother has 'handy enough flour,' but no tea or molasses. The owner is looking after Newfoundland Fishing Rooms, for which he gets flour, tea, molasses, and firewood for the winter. The people assure me that one man, who was aboard the *Strathcona* last fall just as we were going south, starved to death, and many more were just able to hold out till spring. The man who died, they tell me, ate his own dog as his last resource."

Although his main work was with the white fishermen, Grenfell sometimes came across Indians and Eskimos, and was able to help them, too. On one occasion, when they were anchored in Davis Inlet, a band of Indians came to visit the trading-post. They were extremely interested in the steamer, and after getting over their first fears, they would have given all they had to buy the ship's steam whistle and the distress rockets. Among the clothes aboard, Grenfell found a fox-huntsman's red tailcoat, a rather torn red golf blazer and a cavalryman's white Eton coat with silver buttons and badge. The Indians were allowed to hold a rifle shooting match, and were given these clothes as prizes. The winners were extremely proud of themselves in their new finery.

8

❖◆❖◆❖◆❖◆❖◆❖◆❖◆❖◆

How the Work in Labrador
Developed

AFTER TWO YEARS, Dr. Grenfell and his friends found that they needed a great deal more money to equip and maintain their new hospitals. They hated to beg, and would have preferred facing Arctic storms, ice, and fog any day, but there seemed to be no other way.

So at the end of the second year's work, Grenfell sent the *Albert* home to England without him, and the *Princess May* was docked at St. John's for the winter. Then, together with Dr. Bobardt, the young Australian from the hospital at Battle Harbour, he visited Canada to raise money. To Grenfell's horror, his colleague insisted on interviewing all the most prominent people: the Prime Minister, the Governor, the President of the Board of Trade, the University Governors and the leading clergymen. They were received with great kindness

74

and were passed on from city to city with full introductions. Committees were formed, and their tour was extremely successful.

One of the most important people they met was Sir Donald Smith (later Lord Strathcona), who was President of the Hudson's Bay Company. He had lived, as a poor boy, for some years in Labrador, and was therefore particularly interested in the work Dr. Grenfell was doing. His support in the following years was to prove of great importance.

At one of the Canadian meetings, Sir Donald was invited to act as chairman. In order to save expense, Dr. Bobardt sat at the entrance to take the money. When Sir Donald arrived, Bobardt insisted on charging him fifty cents to enter. Sir Donald said that he was the chairman of the meeting, but the Australian replied that several other people had tried to get in free by saying the same thing. When Grenfell later explained that Bobardt did not recognize him, Sir Donald said that he was delighted to find them so businesslike.

Sir Donald insisted that the two young doctors should take a holiday, traveling at his expense on the Canadian Pacific Railway to British Columbia. He arranged for them to ride on the footplate of the engine as it went through the Rocky Mountains, and when they reached Winnipeg, they stayed at Sir Donald's house, where a great welcome had been arranged for them.

Sir Donald later presented the Mission with a fine, fully equipped little steamer, which was named the *Sir Donald*.

Grenfell returned to England in March, 1894, and after a short visit to his fishermen friends in the North Sea, once more made preparations for his return to Labrador. Dr. Bobardt had entered the Royal Navy, and Dr. Curwen, from the hospital at Indian Harbour, had sailed to China for the London Missionary Society. In their places, Dr. Willway and Dr. Bennett, with the two nurses, sailed direct to Labrador in the *Albert*.

Grenfell and an engineer friend, W. B. Wakefield, traveled to St. John's, where they fitted out the *Princess May* and sent her to join the *Albert*. Then they crossed to Montreal, to fetch the *Sir Donald*. They were delighted indeed with the graceful lines and seaworthiness of the new steamer and set out to follow the *Princess May*. On the way, they stopped to visit the sick and hold services, and the doctor performed operations. They had a good voyage and were fast nearing Battle Harbour, with flags flying and brasses polished, all ready for a triumphal entry, when they ran aground on a shoal. A great hole was made in the side, the propeller and shaft were damaged, the keel was splintered, and the ship was left high and dry. Crestfallen and sad, the crew crept ashore, borrowed a boat and rowed to tell their friends at Battle Harbour the bad news. Volunteers dragged the

Sir Donald off the rocks, and the *Albert* carried out the difficult task of towing her three hundred miles to St. John's, where she was put in dry dock and repaired.

Dr. Grenfell cruised north that year in a twenty-foot jolly-boat. He had to depend on the fishermen and settlers for food and lodging, and he learned to know and love them better than he had ever done before. He wrote later in *A Labrador Doctor*:

"I could not help feeling how much more sacrifice they gladly and freely made for me than I should have dreamed of doing for them had they come as visitors to my house in London. I have sailed the seas in ocean greyhounds, and in floating palaces, and in steam yachts, but better than any other voyage I love to dwell on the memories of that summer, cruising the Labrador in a twenty-footer."

The following year, the little *Sir Donald* took Grenfell and his friends far north, where they explored and charted the narrow channels and helped and doctored the fishermen and the settlers. At one time, they were stuck for eleven days in an ice field. The mail-steamer, which was also trapped, had broken her propeller. She appealed to the *Sir Donald* for help. The *Sir Donald*, whose mastheads scarcely reached the decks of the huge mail steamer, carefully nosed her way through the dangerous and heavy pans of ice and gave a tow. After five hours' pulling through breaks in the ice, with men on the ice-pans constantly clearing the rope from the ice pinnacles, the ship was cleared.

The fishermen and settlers who, only a year or two previously, had depended on magic and charms to cure their ills now began to have great faith in the Mission doctors. Their trust in the wise woman and the seventh son of the seventh son began to waver, while stories of the blind men made to see and the cures brought about by operations were on everyone's lips.

There was much pleading for a doctor to remain during the winter. At first this did not seem possible, but Dr. Willway volunteered to stay at Battle Harbour, and, having loaded him with all their spare supplies, the other doctors left him with some anxiety. When they returned the following summer, they watched the coast with real trepidation and anxiety, expecting their friend to be changed and unwell after his privations. When at length a tanned, athletic figure, neat and clean-shaven, leaped over the rail of the ship, they were no longer sympathetic, but envious.

One calamity, however, had overtaken the group; the *Sir Donald,* which had been anchored in one of the near-by bays, had completely disappeared. At first they thought she must have sunk beneath the ice, but dragging and grappling showed no signs of her.

Sometime later, the little ship was picked up three hundred miles away, in the Atlantic Ocean, surrounded by pack-ice and seals. All the ice in the bay must have moved out, carrying the ship with it. The sealers who took the ship in tow told Dr. Grenfell that they found the cabin full of seals, sitting around the table drinking tea. The ship was towed into St. John's Harbour. Here she was put up for auction, most of the proceeds going to the sealers as salvage money.

When Captain Samuel Blandford told Dr. Grenfell stories of his sealing trips, and of the hardships and adventures, and how his three hundred men were isolated without the help of a doctor for two months, the doctor could not resist the challenge. In 1896, he returned to Labrador early, to join the ship *Neptune* in St. John's Harbour.

He found the town crowded with men who had come many miles, hoping to be taken on in one of the sealing ships. A successful sealing season meant a great deal to St. John's, for some £50,000 would be earned, and many families depended on it for their main support during the year.

The *Neptune,* like the other ships, was a barque-rigged ship with engines. She was very massive, with sides eighteen inches thick, sheathed and resheathed with greenheart to withstand the battering of the ice. Inside, she was lined with oak and beech. She was double-stemmed, and needed this enormous strength for battering her way through the ice.

Below decks, every corner was adapted for carrying fuel, together with stores of all kinds and food for the crew of three hundred and twenty men.

In order to protect the young seals, no ship was allowed to sail before 2 P.M., on March 14. When this time came, the ships steamed out of the harbor with flags flying, whistles blowing and men cheering from the decks and wharves.

Sealing was a very dangerous occupation, and many men were killed each year. In order to hunt the seals, the men had to land on the ice, and incidents like the following were not unusual. Sixteen men were on the ice in Trinity Bay when the wind changed and the ice was driven off shore. When night came, with a bitter gale blowing, they knew that they had little chance of reaching shore. They were lightly clad and had no fire or food, but they managed to keep alive for thirty-six hours, dragging their boats ten miles over the ice to the land.

As the sealing-ships moved through, the ice watchers in the barrels at the mastheads kept a sharp lookout. When seals were sighted, the sealers would leap from the moving ship onto the ice, and then, leaping from ice-pan to ice-pan, they would run for their prey. When they had killed, pelted and sculped the seals, they would have to begin their perilous return to the ship over the broken ice.

The men often cut themselves painfully or sprained

wrists or ankles, and many suffered from snow-blindness, so Dr. Grenfell was kept very busy.

Whenever he had time, the doctor would go out on the ice with the men. He tells how, on one occasion, he slipped over the side of the boat late in the afternoon, but the ice was loose packed, and he and a dozen other men found themselves isolated on a piece of floating ice, with the ship well out of sight.

They kept warm by playing leap-frog and hop, skip, and jump, and ate sugar and oatmeal mixed with snow. They burned their wooden seal-bat handles with seal fat, making a blaze to attract their ship's attention. When the vessel finally picked them up, late that night, the captain gave them the "blowing-up" of their lives. Later, he told the doctor that he was so relieved to see them safe that he didn't stop to think what he was saying.

When the sealers were unwell, they would lie up in any odd corner of the ship they could find, and when Dr. Grenfell made his daily rounds, he often had great difficulty in finding them. He would take the steward with him, carrying candles and matches. They would search the four main holds, scrambling over barrels and sacks and poking into recesses, and even then they would miss one or two. Although the holds were damp and dirty, the men seemed to be very healthy, probably because of the good food, especially the fresh seal-meat.

The enormous pans of ice battering the sides of the

Neptune made a terrifying noise below decks, and all hands were glad to know that there were thirty-six inches of hardwood between them and the sea.

During this voyage, one ship got caught between the frozen shore ice and the immense floes brought in by the north wind. The ship's sides were crushed in. The men saved what they could, but as soon as the wind dropped and the ice parted, the ship sank like a stone. The men, carrying their kit, marched to the shore over the ice. Walking, rowing and camping, they had a hundred miles to go before reaching their homes.

Sunday was a rest day, when no sealing was allowed. Dr. Grenfell had taken a number of hymn-books with him, and on fine days the crew would sit on deck and enjoy singing together.

In 1897, Dr. Grenfell was asked to sail to Iceland to see what help could be given to the fishermen there. He passed the summer investigating the need for a Mission steamer. He spent the winter in the North Sea, developing and extending the work among the fishermen. During the summer of 1898, he carried out pioneer care among the Irish fishermen.

Meanwhile, the work in Labrador was being carried on and developed by Dr. Willway and other willing workers. During 1897, Grenfell was advised to take a holiday and he stayed in the Scilly Isles with Sir Frederick Treves.

One of his fellow-guests was the novelist A. E. W. Mason. During a regatta, Mason dressed himself up as an old lady and pretended to fall off the end of the pier. Grenfell, disguised as a clergyman, jumped in to rescue him. There was great excitement as they were both dragged out of the water. Mason lost his shirt, and, clad only in a bonnet and blouse over his bathing-suit, rushed for the boathouse. The local newspapers wrote it all up very seriously as a genuine rescue.

9

Labrador Again

IN THE AUTUMN of 1899, Grenfell crossed the Atlantic once more, sailing in an empty ore-tanker as purser. After various adventures, he reached Battle Harbour late in October. Writing to his mother, he said:

"We have just steamed into Battle Harbour, and guns and flags gave us a welcome after our three years' absence. The hospital was full and looked splendid. What a change from the day, now seven years ago, when we first landed! What an oasis for patients from the bleak rocks outside! I never thought to remain long enough in this country to see it."

Grenfell had received many pathetic letters, pleading for help for the dwellers on the North Coast of Newfoundland. These people were very poor and often came near starvation during the winter months.

It was decided to use St. Anthony as a wintering-place for the Indian Harbour staff, beginning medical work in October and closing in June, when the staff could return to Indian Harbour.

A room was hired in a trader's cottage and a large cupboard was prepared to use as a surgery. Arrangements were made for the medical staff to visit a number of villages in the district. These visits, however, soon became impossible because patients began to come in and lodge in near-by cottages, and the serious cases could not be left without constant care. To help them, the doctors found a local motherly woman and trained her to look after some of the patients.

Grenfell enjoyed that first winter. He welcomed the chance to get to know the people better and to help them. He also got much enjoyment from dog-driving.

The real Labrador dog is very like a wolf. He is often two feet four inches high and six feet six inches from the tip of his nose to the tip of his tail, and weighs about a hundred pounds. He has thick, straight hair and pointed ears that always stand up. His long, bushy tail curves over on his back and is always carried erect. He is generally tawny in color like the gray wolf, and has no special markings.

One settler used to tell how he saw his team of dogs mix with a pack of wolves. He could not shoot for fear of killing his own dogs by mistake.

The Eskimo dog never barks. He howls like a wolf, sitting with his head up. The dogs are fearless and, unlike wolves, will attack even the largest polar bear.

Cold does not seem to affect them. They will lie on the ice at fifty degrees below zero and sleep comfortably.

They can climb out of the sea with ice forming all over their coats and be quite unharmed.

The dogs were not at all well behaved, and Dr. Grenfell tells how, on one occasion, he was visiting a patient when the dogs smelled the dinner that was being prepared inside the house. When the door was opened, the dogs rushed into the house like an avalanche, sweeping the doctor off his feet. They knocked the stew-pot off the fire and began a savage fight over its contents. To make matters worse, they burned their noses and seemed to blame one another for the pain. The house was filled with steam, while the Eskimo owner, using a stout harpoon handle and shouting at the top of his voice, tried to drive the dogs out.

Grenfell also tells how, on another occasion, he arrived at a patient's house and found that no food was available for his dogs. His patient, who was too ill to go out of doors, begged the doctor to lock up any vicious dogs because he had a sheep. Grenfell had an excellent dog called Kite, who weighed eighty pounds and had an enormous appetite, so he shut him in a shed. In the morning, the patient was much better and came out to see the doctor off. Grenfell went to open the door of the shed, but the patient cried, "Don't open that door! My sheep is in there." Grenfell went into the hut. No sheep was to be seen. Kite lay smiling on some hay. He weighed over a hundred pounds and could not walk. He had to be left behind.

The dogs pull their loads on komatiks, flexible sledges, which can move over rough ground without upsetting or buckling.

The tracks were often very rough. Dr. Grenfell once spent a whole day covering five miles, while on another day he did seventy-five miles. In clear country, the dogs are expected to do about six miles an hour.

Fortunately, the dogs are good pathfinders. Dr. Grenfell once had to go seventy miles across country. He did not know the trail, but his leading dog had been that way once before. He left it to the dog, and they did the journey in twelve hours, including a one-and-a-half-hour stop for rest and lunch.

Care was taken to assure that the dogs were treated well, and in order to give men a pride in their dogs and teach them how to handle them properly and humanely, dog-team races were organized. These events were very popular and aroused great enthusiasm.

A gun and an ax were essential to all travelers, the gun to shoot game or protect them against polar bears, and the ax for getting to water under the ice or clearing the track in rough country.

In order that one may keep warm in the Labrador winter, clothing has to be made of special materials. Grenfell cloth is one of these. It is impervious to wind and water; it is light in weight, tough, and smooth on the outside so that snow does not stick to it.

The collar of any outside garment has to be carefully

designed so that the cold cannot get in. The edging around the face is trimmed inside and out with fur, and is pulled tight with string threaded through a hem. A rubber band closes an inset in the sleeves, and long gloves come up to the elbow. The trousers, in one piece, reach up to the armpits. Light sealskin boots are best if it is at all wet, but in a dry, cold season, deerskin foot-wear, dressed very soft, is better because it is warmer.

Grenfell found the settlers were very kind to him everywhere. One night he was caught in a blizzard, and it was after midnight when his dogs got him to a tiny cottage. He hammered at the door and woke the owner. The door opened, and he was blown inside by the storm. The owner slipped on some clothes and went out and fed the dogs. His wife lit the fire and made some hot cocoa with milk and sugar. It was only much later that Gren-fell realized that this came from a carefully guarded hoard kept for visitors only. He was then sent to bed while the owners slept on the floor nearby. They would take nothing at all in return for their hospitality.

In another case, Grenfell's host started out before him in the morning, to make the fourteen-mile trail to the next village and also to give the new host there some milk and sugar because he was too poor to have any himself to entertain the doctor.

On these trips Grenfell often had to perform serious operations under the most primitive conditions. In one case, he was called out to see a boy with a broken thigh. He arrived at midnight, and his first job was to thaw out a piece of frozen board to make splints. He gave chloroform and set the limb. In the morning, he was awakened by his patient singing and talking to his dog.

On one of these journeys, Grenfell, in order to save time, tried to take a short cut across a harbor. The ice gave way, and he fell into the chilly water and was drenched to the skin. He scrambled out, but he knew that, unless he changed his clothes, he would very likely be frozen to death. He shouted to his companion to drive to a small wood, while he followed as quickly as possible. His clothes were soon frozen hard, and he felt like a man running in heavy armor. When he reached the trees, he was able to scramble into his dry clothes. He was none the worse for this adventure.

On several occasions, the doctor lost his way in the fog and snow and was unable to find the huts which were built along the tracks for travelers in distress. Once, when he ran out of food, he was driven to chewing pieces of green sealskin cut from his boots and to boiling his skin gloves over a fire.

Sometimes, when he needed food, he would do some hunting on these trips. He was crossing a bay once when he saw some seals in the water, just off the edge of the ice. Podge, his leading dog, was a seal hunter, so, unhitching him, Grenfell crept out to the edge and laid himself flat on the ice. There he waited, occasionally lifting and waggling his leg, just as a seal wags its tail. The seals, full of curiosity, approached, and Grenfell was able to shoot two of them. Podge recovered them, and they made a much-needed meal for the dogs.

In the spring of 1900, the new and specially built hospital steamer, the *Strathcona*, crossed the Atlantic in ten days and picked up Grenfell to begin his work once more among the fishing fleets of the Labrador coast, so the work at St. Anthony was closed down for the summer.

The new steamer took the staff farther north than they had ever been before. They had with them one of the Moravian Brethren, who was anxious to find a suitable place to build a new station so that they could help Eskimos who had previously been too far off to be reached.

The uncharted, narrow waterways often made their journey very perilous. When they turned southward once more, they visited numerous harbors, where there were always many fishermen and settlers anxious to consult them.

The doctor's work was made much more difficult because the patients frequently found it hard to describe their ailments. One man said that he was "chilled to the conders." A women said her complaint was "too turrible to tell." The doctor also had to be particularly careful in his prescriptions. He gave one woman liniment for her stiff knee, and, because it was so successful, she took a good dose to cure her stomach-ache. Quite often, too, when the doctor ordered "one teaspoonful, three times a day" a patient would take the whole lot in one gulp, believing that he would be cured all the quicker.

When the winter began, Grenfell returned to St. Anthony and once more opened his surgery in the cottage. There were now so many patients that in the spring Grenfell had to tell the people round about that it was impossible for him to carry on without a hospital.

At once, an expedition into the woods was arranged, with a hundred men and three times as many dogs. They camped among the trees and began felling. Grenfell, who was no axman, undertook to supply the food. He calculated how much he would need by taking the amount a hundred convicts on hard labor in England would eat in two weeks. He was astounded to find that his hundred hungry men ate it all in one day!

At the end of a fortnight, they came home hauling sufficient logs for a hospital building thirty-six feet by thirty-six feet.

The hospital opened six months later, and, together with enlargements, lasted until 1927, when it was replaced by a large fireproof building.

In 1901, Dr. Grenfell and his friends had a great deal

of trouble with a man who persisted in selling intoxicating drinks near one of their hospitals. They had many arguments with this man, but they could do nothing to stop him.

That summer, when Grenfell was steaming north to one of his hospitals, he picked up three men in a small boat who claimed that their steam launch had been wrecked. This well-insured boat belonged to the seller of intoxicants. When the three men had told their story, Grenfell steamed as close to the wreck as possible. He planned, as Lloyd's agent, to make an examination of it.

The three rescued men became very nervous and even tried to row off to the wreck. On examination, Grenfell and his friends found that the water was pouring into the boat through a round hole. They made a bung from a tree trunk, pumped out the water and soon had her floating alongside. They towed her to the owner's landing-stage. He was awakened and induced to sign a document selling the little steamer to Grenfell for fifty cents. To the latter, this was as good as a confession that the storekeeper had attempted to sink the steamer in order to claim the insurance money.

The boat was towed south and properly surveyed, and there was no doubt that she had been deliberately holed. But while being towed back to St. John's, the boat sank, and vital evidence was lost.

A year or two later, as winter was setting in and Grenfell was about to sail for England, word came that a large ship had been lost near the store of the seller of intoxicants. The skipper and the mate of the wreck reported that they had been forced to leave the ship and that they had sold her for eighty dollars to the store-keeper.

The place was six hundred miles north, and it was November, but Grenfell felt that there might be a chance of saving the wrecked vessel. He hired a steam trawler and set off that night.

Ice formed thickly over the whole ship, and they took a long time to locate the position of the wreck in the drifting snow. They had to cut through ice to reach the wrecked vessel, but when they did so they found that there was nothing at all wrong with her except that all her movable equipment had been taken out.

In the store on the beach nearby, they found all the ship's gear. In a very short time, they had her fully equipped, with a skeleton crew on board. After many adventures, they reached St. John's safely. The captain and the owner had left for England, but they were extradited and finally sent to prison.

10

Trading

THE EVILS of the truck system were obvious to Grenfell from his earliest days in Labrador, and it was inevitable that the time must come when he would have to lead the attack upon it.

The settlers and the fishermen took everything they caught or trapped to the merchants. In exchange, they received stores, tools, clothes and equipment. No money changed hands, and each settler or fisherman ran an account in which his credits or debts were shown. If there was a bad season or the man was unlucky, he became heavily in debt to the company. In addition, the merchants charged high prices for essential goods, so that it could happen that a sack of flour worth sixteen shillings would be put down in an account at thirty shillings.

If a man dared to sell his fish or furs elsewhere, his own merchant would demand to have his debts paid and refuse him essential goods for the winter.

In time, the system killed initiative, because men whose supplies were cut off simply applied for Government relief and charity.

As Dr. Grenfell reported:

"Hitherto lack of experience had compelled us to cope with this evil of hunger and nakedness by collecting and distributing clothing, and helping the people in various ways to get food. Now we realized the futility of giving financial help to men who had to pay twelve shillings for a hogshead of salt which could be bought at St. John's for four shillings. We were vigorously stirred by the fact that many of our most piteous cases of tuberculosis of glands and bones were the direct result of chronic semi-starvation, notably amongst the children."

During Grenfell's fifth season in Labrador, there was a financial crisis in which Newfoundland's two banks failed; ten out of twelve merchants' firms could not pay their way, and most of the population faced ruin. This was the direct result of a bad fishing season and the working of the truck system. The crash, however, had one good result in that Canadian banks took over and reorganized trade and industry so that some of the worst evils were swept away.

In spite of the warnings of merchant friends, Grenfell believed that co-operative trading, run by the settlers themselves, was the solution to the problem. His first venture began in Red Bay, on the north side of the Straits of Belle Isle. He called there one autumn and found the fishermen waiting for him so that they could beg a passage south, as they could no longer make a living. He gathered them together, and after a long discussion, they decided to set up as their own merchants, sharing the risks and dividing the profits.

The seventeen families had only eight-five dollars between them, so Grenfell had to lend them the money to buy their first shipload of stores. The fishermen were so afraid of the merchants that they did not want their names pubished, and they were even opposed to putting up a sign outside their store. Grenfell, however, insisted on chalking in large letters across the front of the building: "RED BAY CO-OPERATIVE STORES."

When supplies were received, it was found that they could be sold at half the prices charged by the merchants.

This co-operative effort was so successful that within a few years the inhabitants of Red Bay were out of debt, and they were never again in danger of starvation, even when there was a bad fishing season.

The success of this store caused similar stores to be opened elsewhere. The trading companies reacted by demanding an inquiry into the Grenfell Association, claiming that it was "a menace to honest trade." A commission was appointed and the inquiry made. The result was a complete vindication of the Association and the best advertisement it could possibly have had.

As time went on, bigger stores were opened and made large profits. But progress was not smooth, and at one time Dr. Grenfell found himself personally responsible for a debt of twenty-five thousand dollars, which a manager of one of the stores had contracted through inefficiency. In order to clear this debt, Dr. Grenfell had to sell everything he possessed.

As another means of helping the poorer settlers, Grenfell decided to set up a sawmill in Canada Bay, about sixty miles south of St. Anthony. This was no easy venture. Although the Government gave a special grant, the main expense fell on Grenfell personally. He and his friends knew nothing about sawmills, neither had they seen the proposed site for the mill. However, they ordered the mill from England and arranged for two young Englishmen, who had volunteered for the job, to come and help them set it up.

When Grenfell found that one of the boilers weighed three tons, he spent a great deal of time worrying about how it could possibly be landed from the Mission schooner.

The project had more than its share of troubles, for at first the workmen could not get the machinery to operate because part of it had been installed upside-down! But the second year was even more critical because the firms which had bought the timber from the mill did not pay the bills in time for the winter supplies to be bought and sent to the loggers.

When supplies were finally obtained, the bay was frozen over, and they had to be unloaded nine miles from the mill. They were then loaded onto the little hospital steamer *Strathcona*. By piling all the stores at the after end of the ship and steaming forward so that the bow ran onto the ice and then broke through it, they were finally able to reach the mill.

A visit across country to the mill was hazardous because no one knew the way, and where the snow lay deep over the tops of the trees and bushes and ravines, it was very dangerous, for it would suddenly collapse, and a man could sink in and be suffocated.

Dr. Grenfell and some friends were very eager to visit the mill. He later wrote in *A Labrador Doctor:*

"We hoped to reach the mill in two days, but at the end of that time we were still trying to push through the tangle of these close-grown forests. To steer by compass sounded easy, but the wretched instrument seemed to point persistently to precipitous cliffs or impenetrable thickets. There were no barren hilltops after the first twenty miles. Occasionally we would stop, climb a tree, and try to get a view. But climbing a conifer whose boughs are heavily laden with ice and snow is no joke, and gave very meagre returns. At last, however, we struck a high divide, and from an island in the center of a lake, occupied only with two lone fir trees, we got a view both ways, showing the Cloudy Hills which towered over the south side of the bay in which the mill stood.

"A very high, densely wooded hill lay, however, directly in our path; and which way to get round it best none of us knew. We tossed up and went to the eastward—the wrong side, of course. We soon struck a river, and at once surmised that if we followed it, it must bring us to the head of the bay, which meant only three miles of salt-water ice to cover. Alas, the stream proved very torrential. It leaped here and there over so many rapid falls that great canyons were left in the ice, and instead of being able to dash along as when first we struck it, we had painfully to pick our way between heavy ice-blocks, which sorely tangled up our traces, and our dogs ran great danger of being injured. Nor could we leave the river, for the banks were precipitous and utterly impassable with undergrowth. At length we came to a gorge where the boiling torrent was not even frozen, and as prospects of being washed under the ice became only too vivid, we were forced to cut our way out on the sloping sides. The task was great fun, but an exceedingly slow process.

"It was altogether an exciting and delightful trip. . . .

"On the fourth day we reached the mill, to find that logging had progressed satisfactorily, and the future looked rosy for this latest attempt to give work and food and money and self-respect instead of a dole."

Because the fur-trapper's life was so uncertain, **Dr.**

Grenfell decided to try to breed animals for their fur.
A fox farm was started near the hospital at St. Anthony.
They soon had a dozen couples—red, white, and one
pair of silvers. The young pups were very tame, but they
died or their parents ate them. A Harvard professor who
was aboard the *Strathcona* that summer records that
fifteen little foxes were being carried for the farm. As
they had been brought aboard in blubber casks, their
coats were very sticky. After a few days, they became
very tame and played all over the deck. They fell down
the companionway, and were always having their tails
or their feet stepped on, and when they were not yelping
with pain, they were yelling for food.

The poor seaman whose job it was to look after them
said, "I been cleaned out that fox-box. It do be shockin'.
I been in a courageous turmoil my time, but dis be the
head smell ever I witnessed."

As the farm had no success in raising fox pups and a
sickness spread among the other foxes, the operators
decided to abandon the experiment.

Subsequently, a number of fox farms were opened in
Newfoundland and Labrador, and some were very successful.

11

❖❖❖❖❖❖❖❖❖❖❖❖❖❖

Collecting Children and
Educating Them

DR. GRENFELL LOVED children, and he was much distressed
whenever he found boys and girls who, for one reason or
another, could not be cared for by their parents.

One day, an SOS signal from the shore caused Grenfell
and some helpers to visit an isolated little cottage, where
they found a dead woman and a dying man, both the
victims of influenza. There were also five little children.
The next day, after the visitors had buried the father and
mother, they had to take the children with them, and
that began Dr. Grenfell's collection of children.

Another time, Dr. Grenfell and some students looked
into what they thought was an abandoned hut, but they
discovered that there were four starving children in the
loft above the ceiling. Later, a woman carrying a baby
came back to the hut. She had been out to collect berries
to feed the children. She felt that she could carry on no

longer and pleaded with the doctor to take the children and care for them, which he did.

On an early summer voyage, Dr. Grenfell found that a four-year-old girl had been brought in to the Indian Harbour Hospital. While her father was away hunting and her mother was ill in bed, the little girl had crawled out of the house into the snow, and by the time she was found both her legs were badly frozen. They had to be amputated, but the doctors gave her such good artificial limbs that she could finally run and play with the other children. She also joined Dr. Grenfell's collection of children.

In the autumn of that same year, as winter approached, the doctor was told of a family living in great poverty on a small island. A search party started out. At first there seemed to be no sign of life on the island, but they finally saw a thin column of smoke and found that a sheet of light canvas, pegged against the face of the rocks, was the only shelter for six people. There was a mother with a tiny baby, two small boys with practically no clothes, the father, who appeared to be feeble-minded, and another boy of about fifteen years. It had already begun to snow, and eight winter months lay ahead. Grenfell and his first mate sat down to talk to the man and his wife. The man asked for clothing. Grenfell and his mate pleaded with him to let them take some of the children so that they could be cared for. Finally, in return for clothes and stores, the two small boys were grabbed by the sturdy mate, tucked one under each arm, and taken off to the boat, to be added to the collection. Later, Grenfell arranged for the family to be transferred to the mainland and given a decent cabin and a stock of provisions.

One day, a woman came aboard the doctor's boat with a bundle under each arm. She laid these on his chartroom table and untied them: The two children in the bundles were blind. The woman's husband had been killed in an accident, and she had four other children, so she had decided to give the two blind ones to the doctor. He accepted them and added them to his collection. When they were old enough, he sent them to the School for the Blind in Halifax. After they returned, an operation was performed, and they were both given partial sight, so that they could see colors, read large print and distinguish faces.

When it was known that Dr. Grenfell was taking care of orphans and children whose parents could not keep them, his adopted family grew at an alarming rate.

At first, Grenfell found friends willing to adopt the children; then he was forced to send them to England, Canada, or the United States, to children's homes or orphanages.

Eventually, Grenfell managed to raise enough money to build his first Children's Home, at St. Anthony. It had to be built of newly felled timber and accommodated twenty children. It was expanded to meet the needs of the growing family, but the green timber contracted, so the roof leaked, the windows rattled, and the snow blew in around the doors and windows. In spite of its very expensive heating system, the rooms always seemed cold. There was no day nursery for the little children, no isolation room for the sick, no proper storage for food, and the rats and mice were numerous and cheeky.

The ladies who volunteered to come to look after this group of untrained children, some of them crippled or very backward, needed to be very brave. Not only did they have the task of mothering and taming them, but they had to cook on a leaky range, deal with an inefficient heating system and cope with leaking barrels of water which stood in the kitchen and were, for a long time, their only means of obtaining water.

What was really needed was a concrete building, so Grenfell planned one and appealed to people all over the world to contribute twenty-five cents for a brick. Many people gave fittings, local people and students from America worked without wages, and, after two years, the building was finished.

Was all this effort worth while? It is interesting to know that one of the two little naked boys whom Grenfell had exchanged for clothes became a master carpenter; the other became a stores manager. One of the little girls rescued from the cabin where both parents died of influenza became a nurse, and the blind babies were finally able to teach spinning and weaving.

All the money granted by the Government for education in Newfoundland and Labrador was divided among the various religious denominations, so a number of schools were established where one would have been sufficient. This meant a great waste in both buildings and teaching staff. Grenfell and his friends tried to get these schools to combine. When this proved hopeless, they decided that they must open a school of their own. The only building available was very poor—"not so good as the accommodation which we have provided for our pigs," wrote Grenfell—so money had to be raised to put up new buildings.

One of the first things that Grenfell and his friends had noticed in Labrador was the lack of games and toys for the children, particularly the absence of toys. At one time, they brought out and distributed a whole trunkful of dolls, but were astonished to find later that these were nailed high on the wall as ornaments, well out of the reach of the children.

Volunteer teachers and helpers who had been trained in kindergarten work came and helped to introduce organized play. The children, of course, took to it like ducks to water.

At last, enough money was raised to build the new

school. A large hall, which could be used for physical education and entertainments put on by the children themselves, was included, together with a library of several thousand books.

This original school grew until it now has over two hundred children on its roll.

A number of other schools were opened at various places, some of the scholars being permanent and the others returning home during the summer.

The fame of the Grenfell schools spread, and many children traveled long distances to attend them. Grenfell tells how one day he met a very small boy walking down the gangplank of the mail steamer, struggling with a heavy kitbag.

" 'Who are you?' I asked.

" 'I'm Percy.'

" 'Where do you come from?'

" 'North Labrador, sir.'

" 'What have you come to St. Anthony for?'

" 'To get learning.'

"He was a small orphan from a remote village of our northern coast. He had come along with all he owned because he had heard that children would be given a chance at the Grenfell School. Today he is married and doing well as a trapper and fisherman, having had his 'schooling' and returned to his own village in the Far North."

For many years it was not possible to deal with the education of small groups of children in the most isolated settlements. Then a lady teacher, a Doctor of Philosophy, traveled to Labrador at her own expense and stayed in one of the small villages, to teach for the summer. She continued to do this for twenty years and, in addition, built up a band of volunteer teachers who, like her, came each year to remote villages, where they lived with the fisher people and gathered together their pupils wherever they could find a vacant room.

Not the least useful service performed by the hospital steamer was the distribution of library boxes containing about fifty books each. Voluntary teachers and librarians helped to make this service very successful.

The most promising boys and girls in the schools were sent to schools and colleges in England, Canada and the United States, to further and complete their education. It was hoped that they would return to Labrador to help their own people. About eighty per cent did so. They served on the Coast as mechanical engineers, electricians, plumbers, shoemakers, teachers, dressmakers, cabinetmakers, trained nurses, dietitians, stenographers, managers of stores, industrial teachers and clergymen.

In *A Labrador Doctor,* Grenfell wrote:

"Today, after forty years, we have orphanage-boarding-schools at four widely separated centers, where any child can be brought. From this flotsam and jetsam of a barren Coast, with 'nothing worthy to offer mankind,' have come some of our most efficient and loyal helpers. The students of Yale University are responsible for one of these centers, Princeton for another and friends in Chicago for a third, while St. Anthony Orphanage is a truly international effort.

"We rejoice to reflect that the problems of the underprivileged children in Labrador can be solved as long as our schools and orphanages carry on. The one test for efficient surgery in these practical days is its 'end results.' Surely that is God's test for our lives. Certainly it is not only the gauge of the value of the outlay in child life, but its justification and, in nine cases out of ten, its more than satisfying reward."

12

❖◆❖◆❖◆❖◆❖◆❖◆❖◆❖◆❖

Adventures at Sea

THE SEA HAD a great fascination for Grenfell, and his friends used to say that you never really got to know him until you had sailed with him in the *Strathcona*.

The worse the weather, the more he seemed to like it! He had many escapes from death, and his seamanship and daring were famous, even with the hardened sailors of the Coast. The settlers would often say to each other, "The wind's blowing wonderful hard. This will be sure to bring Dr. Grenfell." Or, as a Newfoundland skipper said, after seeing Grenfell's ship return safely to port following a tremendous storm, "Sure, I don't know 'ow she 'as done it," adding, "The Lord must kape an eye on that man."

People who sailed with Grenfell said that he really did feel that he was specially selected and protected and that God would allow him to survive until his work was done. So, when it was urgent for him to travel, he would sail in spite of the weather, sometimes moving at a hair-raising speed in the thickest fogs.

One daily event which startled visitors aboard Grenfell's ship was his early-morning ritual of hauling up a bucketful of Arctic water and pouring it all over himself. Even more startling perhaps was a variation of this morning bath when the doctor dived from an ice-floe into the ocean, often from as high as forty feet.

Notoriously restless and active, Grenfell rose at dawn, and would stand at the ship's bows, anxious to up-anchor and be away. Friends remember how Fritz, an enormous brown-and-black dog who worshipped his master, would stand with him and sniff the morning air.

Many ships were wrecked on the Newfoundland and Labrador coasts, and although the fishermen and settlers would never pray for a wreck, they did pray that, if there was to be a wreck, it should be in their neighborhood.

Sometimes the wreck seemed almost providential, as when the Mission cattle were so short of food that it looked as if they would not last out the winter, and a steamer with five thousand tons of barley aboard was wrecked on the rocks within a few hundred yards of their barn!

The *S.S. Mexico* ran into the cliffs in Belle Isle in dense fog and sank at once. For many weeks, barrels of flour were being picked up from the sea. Apart from a half-inch of dough coating on the outside, the flour was in excellent condition. Fishermen, using hooks on long poles, poked into the ship's holds, bringing up hams, cheeses, kegs of butter and many other edible things.

The *S.S. Nordfelt,* with a cargo of five thousand tons of coal, was stranded on a reef a mile offshore. The Mission bought hundreds of tons of this coal for its hospitals and steamers, and most of it was brought ashore over the ice by dog-teams.

The *Scotsman,* also wrecked in Belle Isle, carried many bales of plush, cretonnes and silks which the fishermen salvaged, with the result that many a simple cottage was prettily bedecked—and many a fisherman's wife, too.

The *S.S. Baucis* was wrecked one winter just as the fishermen were wondering what they were going to do for flour. This ship, carrying five thousand tons of wheat, ran high and dry on a flat reef. All that the fishermen had to do was to go alongside her hull, bore a hole in it with an acetylene burner, and the wheat simply poured out into the "harvesting" boats. The *Strathcona* was filled twice over.

One of the wrecked ships was His Majesty's first-class cruiser *Raleigh,* which remained standing right side up on the rocks for some years. The captain forbade the fishermen to do any salvaging, and even fired a shot at one man who attempted to recover an armchair which was being washed ashore. After eight years, the British

Navy blew her up, and for many years afterward people were collecting and selling brass and copper which had been blasted off her hull.

The most exciting wreck, however, was the *Bay Rupert,* a new Hudson's Bay Company steamer, loaded with all kinds of useful supplies worth about two million dollars. She ran onto an uncharted shoal about fourteen miles out from land.

Grenfell paid frequent visits to this ship, and his helpers salvaged many things of great value to the hard-pressed people on the Coast. There were hardwood sledges, barrels of gunpowder, new guns and rifles, all kinds of food, including cheese, mango chutney, nuts and oranges, and ham and tongue.

In order to help the Eskimos, Grenfell guided a number of them out in their small boats, to get what they could from the wreck. One of the first things he had to do when the natives got aboard was to stop an Eskimo from smashing a box of T.N.T., in order to see what was in it.

On these trips, Grenfell made it his job to stand on the bridge, keep an eye on the weather and see that the Eskimos didn't get into danger. Their selection of things to take ashore was astonishing. Although they were fifteen miles out in the Atlantic, in small boats, they would often take back things like rusty metal from the ship's funnels or twisted iron rails.

Tommy, the cabin boy, was very useful in finding things in the holds of the wrecked ship. He would make tiny burrows and crawl through them to find the most useful cargo. One day, his diligence was rewarded by the discovery of large quantities of chewing-gum and chocolate!

Then, late one afternoon, while Grenfell was aboard the wreck with some Eskimos, a heavy gale broke unexpectedly. The *Strathcona,* with no one aboard was anchored a few hundred yards away. The Eskimos were ordered to make for the land in their small boats. The dory, which was already loaded, headed for the *Strathcona* and, after a furious battle with the rising gale, reached her safely.

The men left on the wreck were in great danger, because at any moment she might be washed off the reef into the sea. They had a small lifeboat alongside and had been trying to lower some very heavy iron blocks into her. From the upper deck, where they were working, the lifeboat looked a mere speck far below. Suddenly, to their horror, the rope holding the iron blocks broke and the blocks fell. They all knew that, if they fell into the lifeboat, it would be smashed, and there would be no chance of getting back to the *Strathcona.* But as the rope parted, a wave shifted the little craft, and the iron blocks fell between the lifeboat and the iron side of the *Bay Rupert.* But their perils were not yet over: an enormous wave brought the lifeboat up the side of the *Bay Rupert,* and her bow became fast in a loop hanging from the deck. When the wave went down, the lifeboat was left dangling high in the air. If she fell out of the loop, she would certainly capsize and sink. But by a miracle the very next wave swept up the side of the *Bay Rupert* and freed the lifeboat, laying her on the water right side up. The men finally got away from the wreck, but, as they had only two old oars, picking up the *Strathcona* was a perilous task. At last, they scrambled aboard and, wishing to save the lifeboat, towed her, although she was full of water. She kept afloat because of her two air-tanks.

With the storm growing more and more violent and the darkness becoming more and more intense, Grenfell and his crew set about the task of shepherding in the Eskimo boats, the drag of the submerged lifeboat helping rather than hindering them.

All the boats made for a tiny safe harbor, which had one big drawback—its entrance was only a little wider than their ship. It was no more than seven fathoms deep, and the channel was not straight. All the boats made this harbor safely, however. They stayed there five days, until the gale blew itself out.

When the storm was over, the salvage operators climbed up the cliffs and saw that, at last, the wreck had gone below.

The *Strathcona* had one of her narrowest escapes early one summer when a sudden breeze drove in an enormous ice-floe which pinned her tight against the shore ice. As the pressure increased, the ice seemed to be melting away, so the shore rocks came nearer and nearer. In addition, the vessel was being swept directly toward a rocky headland. As if this were not enough, one of the flanges broke off the propeller. When the cape was only a few yards away and it seemed that the ship could not avoid the rocks, the crew put a small boat, containing some food and blankets, on the ice alongside. But a sudden twist swept the ship past the dangerous rocks and carried it out into the open Atlantic. They were glad to have lost only their small boat.

In the early days, there was not a single lighthouse on this dangerous coast, and many boats were needlessly lost. The fishermen's craft were small and difficult to handle because their decks were cluttered with all kinds of gear, so it was their custom to creep up the coast close inshore and dart into a harbor before darkness fell.

Grenfell complained again and again about the lack of lights along the coast, but the Government would do nothing about it. Finally, he raised a subscription to have a light placed near Battle Harbour. When the plans for building the light were almost complete, the Government forbade it. Eventually, they built one themselves.

At Indian Tickle, there was great need for a light,

because all the fishing schooners passed that way. One autumn, Grenfell was sailing south with the fishing fleet, hoping to put in at Indian Tickle for the night, when a thick fog closed down on them. As they were inside the reefs, the only safe thing to do was to drop anchor. When there was a rift in the fog, they saw eleven lights around them and hoped that they had made the harbor.

As night fell, the strong wind increased and great seas began to heave in. Soon the anchors were straining and mountainous seas were washing over the decks. The patients aboard were dressed and the small boats prepared for launching. Gradually, one after another, the riding lights of the other boats disappeared.

When daylight came, there was only one fishing boat left, and this was drifting toward the reefs. As those aboard the hospital ship watched, aghast, she touched a reef and turned on to her side. The hospital ship, by steaming to her anchors, was saved, but all the other vessels went ashore and were completely wrecked.

As it grew lighter they could see the shore, but before they were able to get their anchors up, there was trouble with the main steam-pipe, and the engines had to be stopped. The engineers worked furiously to repair the damage before darkness came again, knowing full well that on them depended the lives of all aboard. In the afternoon, just in time, the chief engineer was able to give the signal to go ahead once more.

The Government later put a fine light on White

Point, at the very place where the hospital ship anchored on that tragic night.

Close to the hospital at Indian Harbour was a narrow passage known as the White Cockade, and through this the fishing fleet had to pass. There was great need for a light here, and Grenfell sought permission to erect the light which had been planned for Battle Harbour. The Government forbade this, but later put one up themselves. The fishermen were not slow in suggesting that Grenfell's light should be offered somewhere fresh each year.

On Saturday, July 28, 1908, a hurricane began. The hospital ship was anchored in a shallow and unsafe roadstead about twenty miles from the hospital at Indian Harbour. As the barometer was dropping and those aboard were suspicious of the weather, they kept a special watch, at midnight got up steam, and by the first glint of daylight they were anchored in the narrow harbor in which the hospital stands.

The wind increased in fury during the day, and all the fishing boats in the harbor filled and sank. As the weather grew worse, the hospital ship got up steam and steamed to her anchors to ease the strain on the chains and shore lines. By Sunday night, the worst of the storm was over, and on Monday there was a flat calm, with lovely sunshine, but with an enormous, sullen ground sea.

Hoping to help friends in trouble, the hospital ship

got under way and sailed north, keeping as close inshore as possible, while those aboard watched through glasses. Wreckage littered the coast. Forty-one ships had been lost, and on one stretch of coast, about forty miles from Indian Harbour, they discovered sixteen wrecks. Here they also found shelters made from wreckage and women busy cooking meals.

The Grenfell group decided that only one ship, the *Pendragon,* was worth saving. They bought her from her owner at an auction on the beach. They had great difficulty in getting her back into the sea, and when they did so, they found that she was leaking badly. Pumps kept her afloat until they were able to draw her topsail under her. At one point, Grenfell was so tired that he said they might as well let her sink, but two of his crew volunteered to pump all night and kept her afloat.

As the salvage party hunted for a crew to take the *Pendragon* south, they came across the wreck of a new boat which had been launched only two months earlier. They were so sorry for the skipper that they handed over the *Pendragon* to him for what it had cost them at the auction.

The hospital steamer sailed back to Indian Harbour with fifty people aboard and towlines pulling nineteen fishing boats. The mission staff did what they could for these people until the steamer came to take them south.

Charts of the coast were non-existent, and Grenfell

was very eager to have a reliable survey made. The Governor, His Excellency Sir William MacGregor, who was an expert surveyor, came to Labrador and spent a short time helping to chart the North Coast.

The charts were finally accepted by the Royal Geographical Society, who in 1911 awarded Grenfell the Murchison Prize for outstanding achievement in the fields of geography and geology.

13

◆◆◆◆◆◆◆◆◆◆◆◆◆◆◆◆◆◆◆

The Ice-Pan Adventure

ON EASTER SUNDAY in 1908, Dr. Grenfell was called out to attend to an urgent case, sixty miles to the south. He started at once, with his komatik pulled by an especially good team of dogs—Moody, Watch, Spy, Doc, Brin, Jerry, Sue and Jock. Fog and rain had softened the snow, and traveling was difficult. He covered twenty miles, then stopped overnight at a village on the edge of a bay where a heavy sea was heaving the ice into the shore.

Next morning, rain began to fall, and traveling was even more difficult because the rough sea of the previous night had broken up the surface ice and huge ice-pans were breaking away. Half a mile out, there was open water.

In the middle of the bay, about three miles from the shore, there was a small island. This was still connected to the land with ice, and, although the ice was cracked here and there, Dr. Grenfell succeeded in reaching it.

There was now about four miles to go to reach the opposite shore.

The ice looked rough where it had been piled up by the sea, but it seemed safe enough. All went well until the dogs were about a quarter of a mile from the shore. Then the wind dropped, and Grenfell realized that they were traveling over soft ice. An offshore wind sprang up, and the whole field of ice that had been pressed inshore by the east wind began to break up.

At once, Grenfell dragged off his oilskins and threw himself on his hands and knees beside the komatik. He shouted to the dogs to make a dash for the shore, but they had gone only twenty yards when, scenting danger, they hesitated, and at once the komatik sank. The dogs pulled harder but sank in themselves. Grenfell cut their traces, winding the leader's trace around his wrist. By now, they were all in the water, with no ice nearby that was likely to hold them. The leading dog managed to scramble onto a large piece of frozen, hard-packed snow. Having shaken the ice and water from his shaggy coat, he turned and looked at the others still in the water, and the black markings on his face made him look as though he were grinning with satisfaction.

Grenfell hauled himself slowly toward the snow-raft by means of the trace. He was nearly up to it when the leader turned and slipped out of his harness.

Grenfell now began to feel drowsy with the cold, but

he noticed the trace of another dog near by, and at last managed to drag himself and the other dogs onto the snow. But their little raft was so small it was obvious that they would all be drowned if they stayed on it, for it was being driven toward the open sea.

Twenty yards away was a large and firm pan of ice, and Grenfel decided that they must reach it. He took his hunting knife, which he had tied to the back of one of the dogs, and spliced the dogs' sealskin traces into one long line. Then he divided this into two parts, fastening two of the ends to the backs of two of the dogs and the other two ends to his own wrists. His sealskin boots, which reached up to his hips, were full of ice and water. He took these off and fastened them on the dogs' backs. He had already lost his coat, cap, gloves and overalls.

But, try as he might, Grenfell could not get the dogs to swim to the new ice-pan. When he threw them off into the water, they simply scrambled back to him, probably because they could not see the ice-pan when they were in the water.

Finally, the doctor took his black spaniel, which he had with him, showed him the ice-pan and threw a lump of ice onto it. At once, the spaniel, as light as a feather, skipped across the sea ice and lay like a black ball where the leaders could see him. The other dogs now understood what they had to do and struggled bravely to the ice-pan. Then Grenfell ran the length of the little snow-raft and dived, to slither along the surface as far as possible before falling through the ice again. After a long and exhausting fight, he managed to drag himself onto the new pan.

On examination this new pan proved to be compressed snow, which would surely break up as soon as it met the waves. Moreover, it was steadily drifting seaward. The chances of rescue or of even being seen were very remote indeed.

To protect himself against freezing, Grenfell cut down his long sealskin boots as far as the feet and made a kind of jacket to shield his back from the wind.

To the north, he could see enormous pans of ice surging to and fro and thundering against the cliffs. No boat could hope to get through that way.

Grenfell now saw that if he was to live through the night he would have to kill and skin some of the dogs. This was a heart-breaking decision for him to have to make. It was hardly safe to move on the ice-pan, but with great difficulty he succeeded in killing three of the dogs and skinning them.

The hard work left him little time to think about his desperate plight. When night came, he was ten miles out from the bay, wrapped in the dogs' skins. He tried to light a small signal fire, but his matches were soaked and useless. He piled up the carcasses of the dogs to make a windbreak.

Now and again he took off his clothes, squeezed the water out of them, and held them up in the wind. Then he put them on in turn next to his skin, hoping that the heat of his body would dry them.

He had great difficulty in protecting his feet, because his moccasins were so easily soaked through in the snow. In spite of fingers that were more or less frozen, he finally unraveled some of the ropes from the dogs' harness and stuffed the fibres into his shoes.

It happened that Grenfell was wearing some very old clothes, and it amused him to see that he had on his old University running-shorts, red-yellow-and-black football stockings and a flannel shirt.

He now forced the biggest dog to lie down and cuddled up close to him, covered with his dogskins. He slept until midnight, then woke, shivering enough to shatter the ice-pan. The moon was rising, and they were still drifting seaward.

Then a miracle happened: the wind veered and dropped, leaving the sea quite calm. Grenfell turned over and went to sleep again. . . .

When he next awakened, he decided that he must have a flag of some sort. He used his shirt for this purpose.

Occasionally he thought he saw people on the cliffs, but they always turned out to be trees. Once he thought he saw a boat, but it was only another ice-pan.

He was just searching for a piece of transparent ice

which might act as a burning-glass, when he thought he caught the glitter of an oar-blade, but this seemed impossible because there could be little clear water between him and the land. Besides, he had lost his snow-glasses and he was partly snow-blind. But at last there could be no mistake—there was a boat approaching, and the men in it were waving and shouting frantically, much more excited than Grenfell himself.

The first man leaped onto the ice-pan and grasped the doctor's hand without a word, and there were tears in his eyes. Grenfell was given a swallow of hot tea, the dogs were hoisted aboard, and the party started for the shore, rowing in the open parts, pushing pans aside with the oars, and here and there leaping out and pulling the boat bodily over the ice.

On the previous night, four men had been on the headland, cutting up seals. Just as they were leaving for home, one of them had caught sight of the ice-raft and had seen that there was something unusual about it. They went back to the village and reported that there was something living on a drifting floe. A man who owned a spyglass rushed to the cliffs and saw who it was. An attempt was made to launch a boat at once, but the heavy seas made it impossible. At daybreak, a boat was launched in the still dangerous seas.

When the rescue party reached the village, every one turned out to greet the doctor and shake his hand.

News had gone to the hospital that he was lost, so

Grenfell started at once for St. Anthony. The trip was not a pleasant one for him. His feet were so frostbitten that he could not walk, and he had to be hauled home on a komatik. His hands were also badly frozen, and when he got back he had to spend several weeks in bed.

In the hallway of his house he placed a bronze tablet which said:

TO THE MEMORY OF
THREE NOBLE DOGS
MOODY, WATCH, SPY
WHOSE LIVES WERE GIVEN
FOR MINE ON THE ICE
APRIL 21ST, 1908

He loved animals, and his friends say that he never really forgave himself for killing his dogs, even to save himself. It has been said that in later years he suffered nightmares over the killing of these dogs.

The patient whom the doctor had set out to visit was brought into the hospital a day or two after the doctor. He was soon well on the way to recovery.

14

❖—❖—❖—❖—❖—❖—❖—❖—❖—❖—❖—❖—❖

Travel, Exploration and
Communications in Labrador

DURING THE EARLY DAYS in Labrador, the only means of communication during the winter months was by relays of dog-teams from Quebec, and, as might be imagined, mailmen had many exciting and dangerous adventures.

There was an attempt to carry mail across the Straits of Belle Isle. This was extremely dangerous. The narrowest part was nine miles wide, and occasionally violent storms would force millions of tons of ice into the Straits. Enormous masses of ice would grind and smash and ride over one another, making a wild, frightening sight.

One of the mailmen made a strong, light sledge and carried on it a light canvas flatboat which, when necessary, could, in turn, carry the sledge. As it was not possible to make the crossing in one day, he had to sleep out on the ice, which might capsize at any moment and throw him into the frigid sea in pitch-darkness. The

winds and tides were not always predictable, and it is
not surprising that the valiant mailman nearly lost his
life twice by drifting into the Gulf of St. Lawrence. After
four crossings he resigned, and no one was willing, or
able, to take on the job.

The uncertainty and danger of travel in Labrador in
those early days is well illustrated by a trip which Dr.
Grenfell made one spring, starting from St. Anthony.

An important meeting had been arranged in New
York, and Grenfell had planned to go with his dog-team
on the sea ice to the Straits of Belle Isle, then south to
Port Aux Basques, where he could board a steamer for
Nova Scotia, and finally catch a train to New York. This
was usually an excellent, fast route by dog team in the
early spring. But a blizzard blew up, and the heaving
tide under the ice broke it up, making the journey impossible.

The alternative was to risk going south for a hundred
miles by boat, through the broken ice, landing and
walking through the snow for another hundred miles.

When the blizzard blew itself out, Grenfell and a
helper set out in a small motorboat. They had not gone
far before a strong easterly wind began to drive the pack-
ice toward the land, so that there was a real danger that
their boat would be crushed. They headed for the shore,
but ran on a shoal which tore a jagged hole in the hull.
They managed to plug this hole, but the icy wind froze

and burst the pipes in the engine. They landed and built an immense fire of juniper branches to keep themselves warm during the night.

As they could go no farther south, they decided to return to St. Anthony, threading their way between the shore and the ice. Grenfell was already planning to try the route north through the Straits of Belle Isle. They patched up the burst pipes, but it proved impossible to get through the ice, so they ran into a small harbor and borrowed a rowboat from one of the fishermen. They put out to sea again, carefully steering the small boat through the narrow passages between the ice-pans and the shore. Often they had to land on the ice and drag their craft over the pans.

A sudden change of wind brought the ice crashing in toward the shore. Grenfell and his friend leaped out of the boat and tried to drag it onto the ice. They lifted out the bow, but were not quick enough, and the stern was crushed between the ice-pans. The ice-pan upon which they were standing began to drift seaward. They had their guns and a boat hook. They fired their guns to attract attention, but there was no sign of life on the shore.

Grenfell's friend decided to try to get ashore by using the boat hook as a vaulting pole, to leap from ice-pan to ice-pan. He did well until a small pan swayed and he fell into the icy water. Grenfell watched helplessly, fearing that an ice-pan would float over him or that he would become so numb with cold that he would not be able to save himself. But his friend came to the surface, and, after a number of attempts, climbed upon an ice-pan, which promptly began to drift out to sea.

Grenfell, in desperation, fired his rifle again and again, and finally, to his great joy, he saw a boat coming out. It was some fishermen, who rescued both travelers and took them on to St. Anthony.

The meeting in New York had been postponed several times, and Grenfell was more than ever determined to get there. He waited until the ice near the shore had melted, then raised steam in the *Strathcona* and sailed north, planning to go through the Straights of Belle Isle and make contact with the mail-boat.

They found the Straits full of icebergs and pack-ice, so they tried to put back, but it became very cold again and the *Strathcona* was frozen in.

Grenfell now made up his mind to walk. Taking a heavy pack containing food, cooking materials and clothes, he slipped over the side of the *Strathcona* and walked south over the snow and broken ice, sleeping wherever he could find shelter. In three days, he reached a harbor where the sea was open and where the mail-boat was due to call.

Tired but triumphant, he walked to the house of a missionary at the port. He was just sitting down to his first meal when a fisherman rushed in to say that his brother had shot himself in the leg and was bleeding to death. Their hut was five miles away. Grenfell left everything and ran as fast as his tired legs would carry him. He found the young man still alive and stopped the bleeding. He operated on the leg. One of the men who was helping fell in a dead faint as he watched, but the other fortunately managed to carry on, and the young man's life was saved.

Grenfell attended his New York meeting, which had been postponed for two months before it was finally held.

Radio, manned by volunteers, eventually came to be used to keep Labrador in touch with the outside world, and Grenfell was able to report:

". . . on this coast we have sprung into notoriety with our series of Marconi stations, that flash messages from the Straits of Belle Isle as far north as Hamilton Inlet. To the south'ard they are connected with the long line of wires by the Canadian Government along the north side of the Gulf of St. Lawrence. Thus we are in communication with the outside world at last. The object of this wire is to convey information immediately any disaster happens to ships coming to and from Canada."

Later, a regular air-mail service was established.

Grenfell foresaw that Labrador would one day become an important intermediate station for travel between

Europe and America. He was proved right when the world's largest airfield was constructed at Goose Bay. Here, an enormous snow-covered plateau was converted into a landing-ground for the great military aircraft flying between Britain, Canada, and the U.S.A. Gander, the great airfield in Newfoundland, is probably even better known to people flying in commercial airliners.

Damage to ships and boats was a great source of loss to the Labrador fishermen. Crafts were often driven ashore or stranded on the rocks, but it was usually useless to tow them off because the nearest dry dock was hundreds of miles south.

After the hurricane which drove forty-one vessels on to the Labrador rocks, Grenfell had been able to haul off one or two. If a dry dock had been available close at hand, many more could have been saved. But it was obviously useless to haul off a badly damaged ship and try to sail her six hundred miles south in the open Atlantic.

Brave attempts to save ships were made from time to time. One captain, working during low tide, nailed canvas over the inside of a large hole in his ship's bilge, filled up the space with ships' hard biscuit and nailed stout boards on top of the floury mass. He sailed south, keeping his pumps going. The moisture swelled the biscuit and sealed the hole enough to keep him afloat.

One ship which Grenfell helped to haul off the rocks

had her leaking bottom covered with the heavy topsail, into which was dropped peat. The ship was pumped dry, and she was partly patched up inside. Her skipper then sailed her five hundred miles to dry dock.

A very strong appeal was made by Grenfell for a haul-up slip in the north. An anonymous friend gave the money, and, in 1930, a beautiful slip was opened in St. Anthony. On this, vessels up to a hundred and fifty feet could be hauled.

Some people watched this venture sceptically and called it a new "Grenfell Folly," but when five-hundred-ton vessels began to use the slipway, refit and sail away, they were proved wrong. Many ships were saved, and the slipway proved invaluable to the fishermen and sailors of Labrador.

The dock was erected entirely by local people, the only outsider being a professional diver.

In 1927, the boundaries of Labrador were finally defined, and it became more necessary than ever to make charts and maps of the country. Grenfell and his friends therefore decided to give as much time as possible to the making of reliable charts. The first thing they did was to gather together all the charts that had ever been made of the Coast.

The cost of making exact charts was very great, and neither the directors of the Grenfell Association nor Grenfell himself could possibly produce enough money for the undertaking. The British Admiralty wanted to help, but had no ships available. The Canadian Government, too, wished to help, but they could not get permission to land surveying parties.

Dr. Alexander Forbes, a professor at Harvard University, came to Grenfell's aid. He owned a fine schooner and a Waco aeroplane equipped for taking aerial photographs. Commercial firms supplied fuel, workers coming from England were given free passages, the Newfoundland Government gave free passage for materials, and the Geographical Society of New York offered to take all the observations and produce the charts.

To save expense, Dr. Forbes sailed his own vessel. Occasionally he went up in his Waco plane in clear weather, and from the photographs he took he was able to plan a course for his schooner clear of the shoals.

The camera in the floor of the plane was worked by an expert, who took about nine hundred pictures, which covered the parts of the sea and coast to be charted. Dr. Forbes's maps, entitled *Northernmost Labrador Mapped from the Air,* were dedicated to Sir Wilfred Grenfell, "who suggested the project of making a map in Labrador, and whose enthusiasm enhanced the joy of its accomplishment."

Noel Odell, famous for his climbs on Everest, scaled many of the most important Labrador mountains. By the end of 1931, much of the work was completed.

In 1932, the British Admiralty sent out a sixteen-hundred-ton steamer, specially fitted out and sheathed, to complete the survey of the coast of Labrador.

So at last Grenfell achieved his aim of giving his fishermen and sailors the security of reliable charts on this treacherous coast.

15

❖❖❖❖❖❖❖❖❖❖❖❖❖❖

Marriage

IN 1909, Grenfell, having finished a long lecture tour in England, sailed for New York in the *Mauretania*. On board, he became acquainted with a Mr. Stirling, whose daughter was accompanied by a friend. This friend, whom Grenfell came to know as "the girl in black," because she wore black when he met her, attracted him enormously, and he spent much of his time with the group.

The speed with which the *Mauretania* was moving across the ocean made Grenfell fear that he might never see this girl again, so with his usual courage he proposed to her. Her astonished reply was, "But you don't even know my name!" The doctor replied, "That is not the issue; the only thing that interests me is what it is going to be." His answer pleased her, and when the voyage was over he visited her home in Lake Forest, Illinois, and they became engaged. Her name proved to be Anne MacClanahan.

Grenfell returned to St. Anthony, where, amid all his other work, he found time to start building a house which he and his fiancée had planned while they were together at Lake Forest. He chose a spot on the hillside, overlooking the sea and harbor, and, to make sure that the building would be safe in the worst weather, he fastened the main structure to the solid rock foundations with heavy bolts.

In 1909, Admiral Peary returned from his successful expedition to the Pole and put in at Battle Harbour. Grenfell learned of Peary's arrival from a wireless message picked up by his own wireless operator. This was a message from Peary to Washington reporting that he had found the Pole and asking permission to give or sell his remaining stores to the Grenfell Mission. Grenfell at once sent a wireless message to Peary saying GIVE IT TO THEM OF COURSE, signing it WASHINGTON. He knew that Peary would appreciate the joke and that if the supplies had to be paid for, this could be put right very quickly.

When Grenfell reached Battle Harbour he found Peary's party a delightful body of men and enjoyed meeting them all. Among them was Commander Donald MacMillan who later led the Crocker Land expedition.

This same explorer, now Rear Admiral MacMillan, became a great friend of Grenfell's and it was he who began a school for Eskimo children at the most northerly Moravian station at Nain.

Anne Elizabeth Caldwell MacClanahan and Wilfred Grenfell were married in Chicago, in November, 1909. When reporters asked the bride if she really was going to live in Labrador, she replied, "Isn't it usual for a wife to make her home where her husband works?" When Grenfell was asked if he would now, as a married man, take fewer risks, he simply replied, "I must get to my patients."

After a short stay in Hot Springs, Virginia, the couple began their journey north, and sailed from St. John's in January. Grenfell told his wife, who was a good sailor, that she would hardly notice the movement of the ship on this three-hundred-mile trip. But instead of taking the usual five days, they took nine, sailing through gales and blizzards which froze the spray on the ship, making her look like a Christmas cake.

The snow had one good effect; it made their new home look delightful, and as "the girl in black's" furniture had been sent north during the summer everything appeared familiar and comfortable.

The Grenfells had three children, all born at St. Anthony: Wilfred Thomason, born in the autumn of 1910; Kinloch Pascoe, in the autumn of 1912; and Rosamund Loveday, in 1917.

Mrs. Grenfell proved to be a born organizer. She induced many of her friends to give personal help, especially in the Child Welfare Department and in the education work which became her special interest.

Every autumn, she made it her business to see that the boys and girls from Labrador who had scholarships to various educational institutions in America and Canada reached them safely. This was no easy task, for it meant supplying outfits, tickets, routes, personal guides and so on.

Not the least of "the girl in black's" gifts was her ability as a hostess. She kept open house and often entertained large parties of helpers and fishermen.

She was particularly good at suggesting new ways for earning money for the Mission, much preferring honest labor to begging. It was one of her ideas that trucks loaded with Labrador goods to be sold should be driven around holiday resorts by volunteers.

Her sense of humor and fun helped her to triumph over many difficulties. She did not always agree with her husband. His habit of rising with the dawn, for instance, caused her to pin a little notice near the mirror in his cabin on the *Strathcona*. This showed a caterpillar lecturing a group of worms. He was pointing to a bird eating a worm and saying, "Now remember, dear children, the lesson for today—the disobedient worm that would persist in getting up too early in the morning."

Sometimes when Mrs. Grenfell was aboard the *Strathcona* she would chase her husband (or he would chase

her) around the deck, throwing pieces of firewood in a
fast-and-furious mock fight. The big dog Fritz grew
greatly confused, not knowing whether to defend his
master or his mistress.

Grenfell used to write his books, his log and his records
of patients lying face down on the floor of his cabin,
while the ship heaved and rolled in a gale. In better
weather, he would sit on a pile of logs on deck and write.

He would take his scribbled manuscripts home with
him, and Mrs. Grenfell would put these hurried jottings
into some kind of order and prepare them for publica-
tion.

One other way in which the "doctor's woman" gave
him invaluable help was to accompany him on his lecture trips. These tours, which helped to raise money for
the Mission and make its work known, were a great
strain on the doctor. He wrote:

"The actual work and life in the North are an in-
describable rest to both my wife and myself after the
nervous and physical drain of a lecture tour. One used
to wonder at the lack of imagination in those who would
greet us, after long wearisome hours on the train or in
a crowded lecture hall, with 'What a lovely holiday you
are having!' We have learned to regard this oft-repeated
comment only with amusement."

By attending to all the many details of organization,
his wife relieved the doctor of much of the strain of these

lectures. She made all the arrangements for traveling and accommodations and saw that they arrived in time for the lectures. This was not as easy as it sounds because Grenfell was sometimes very absent-minded. During one stay in New York, he stopped to talk with a crossing-sweeper and became so absorbed in the conversation that he quite forgot that there was an audience of three hundred people waiting to hear him lecture. Before leaving the sweeper, he gave him his coat. He never thought much about the clothes he wore, and his wife always had to make sure that he did not turn up for a lecture in his oldest suit.

At the beginning of one lecture on Labrador, he absent-mindedly began talking instead about China and carried on quite oblivious of the frenzied signals being made by his wife. Occasionally, when she saw that the doctor was particularly tired, Mrs. Grenfell would take out some of the lantern slides so that the lecture would not last quite as long as usual.

Grenfell was no orator, but the simplicity and sincerity of his words moved and captivated many great audiences.

Although the lecture tours gave the Grenfells many pleasant experiences, they had to be constantly on the watch that their memories did not betray them. The doctor could not always remember the people he met and sometimes made mistakes. One day a man spoke to him on a train and asked how he liked Toledo. Grenfell said that he had never been there. "That's strange," said the man. "You spent two days in my house there."

Another time Grenfell was introduced to a lady and gentleman, but he did not catch their names. As they did not speak to each other, he thought that he had better introduce them, so he said to the man, "Please let me present you to Mrs. Mmmm," mumbling the name because he did not know it.

"Don't trouble," said the man. "We've been married for thirty years."

Dr. Grenfell's great work in Labrador brought him many honors. Universities conferred degrees on him, learned societies presented him with medals, but the crowning honor came in July, 1927, when Sir William Allardyce, Governor of Newfoundland, representing His Majesty the King, came to open the first modern concrete, fireproof hospital in St. Anthony.

The opening was planned for July 25, and Dr. Grenfell arranged to arrive from a trip north in *Strathcona II* on July 23. But on the way the *Strathcona* ran into dense fog. The ship, moving forward slowly, ran onto a submerged rock and settled on its side. The engineer, in order to prevent an explosion, drew the fires and let off steam. With great difficulty, they got the small boats into the water and tried to heave the *Strathcona* off. But the ship would not move, water was filling the hold, so they decided to try to find land and return the next day to see what they could salvage.

Each man was told to get what he wanted to save before they left. The engineer salvaged a looking-glass and an umbrella. He thought that the umbrella would be useful if they had to land on bare rocks in the rain.

The captain's boat led the way, but in the fog those aboard soon lost sight of the second boat. Suddenly, they heard the sound of a bell. It grew steadily louder, and they thought it strangely like the bell of the *Strathcona*. They made for it, and, to their utter astonishment, the *Strathcona* loomed up in the darkness—afloat!

The other boat was moored alongside. They clambered aboard. The crew of the other boat had heard the bell and rowed back to the ship just in time to see her being washed off the rock by an extra large wave. They went aboard. One man was detailed to ring the bell to attract the captain's attention, while the others began bailing with buckets.

The crew of the captain's boat joined in the bailing. At first it seemed like bailing out the Atlantic Ocean with a spoon, but at last they were able to relight the fires and get the pumps working. There was only a small leak, most of the water having entered through the coal-bunker lids, which were under water when the ship tilted over on the reef.

As the ship began to move, her foghorn attracted the attention of some large fishing boats, which came to their help. The fog was still thick, but Grenfell and his companions decided to risk the passage to St. Anthony.

Two motor-boats piloted them out to sea, then the little ship crept down the coast and hobbled into St. Anthony just before the Governor arrived.

Everything went well, and as all the work of building and installing the equipment had been carried out by Labrador and Newfoundland boys who had returned after training abroad, everyone was especially proud.

Later, this hospital was rated A1 by the American College of Surgeons, who were asked to inspect it.

One central hospital would obviously have been the least expensive way of carrying out work on the Coast, but uncertain transportation made this impossible. It was planned to have a chain of five hospitals, about a hundred and fifty miles apart, with nursing units between each two hospitals, to deal with emergencies. Over the years, after overcoming great physical and financial difficulties, this goal was largely accomplished.

After opening the hospital, His Excellency, to everyone's joy, announced that he had received a cable from His Majesty the King saying that Dr. Grenfell had been created a Knight Commander of the Order of St. Michael and St. George.

16

◆◇◆◇◆◇◆◇◆◇◆◇◆◇◆◇◆

New Developments and
the Reindeer Experiment

THE NEED FOR fresh vegetables for the people of Labrador was always in Grenfell's mind. He was called one day to visit the two sons of an old fisherman. He found these young men, aged twenty and twenty-two, lying helpless, paralyzed from the neck downward. The old father watched anxiously as the doctor carried out his examination. It was the beginning of the fishing season, and he knew that without the help of his sons the family would starve.

The doctor could see at once that the young men had beriberi, a disease which could have been prevented by eating fresh vegetables. It was not the first time that he had seen the results of an inadequate diet in Labrador, and it made him more determined than ever that somehow vegetables must be grown.

He had to face the fact that the soil was poor and the

growing season short. The ground was frozen until July, so seeds could not germinate in time for vegetables to mature. At the beginning, white lice and potato bugs ate and destroyed all the young plants. Grenfell and his workers obtained expert help from an agricultural college in America which sent one of its professors to teach them all the remedies. Later, three Labrador boys were educated at agricultural colleges and returned to help.

American friends presented Dr. Grenfell with some greenhouses, and by July the horticulturists had three-month-old plantlets ready to go into the ground. That autumn, there were many enormous cabbages. It was not long before local settlers were asking for such plantlets themselves, and, in spite of many setbacks, vegetable growing became very popular.

Fishermen were given small amounts of money to purchase seeds and garden tools, and those who could not pay in cash were allowed to work off their loan in the hospital gardens. One man, who had been unable to go fishing, spent the whole summer in his garden. He harvested sixty barrels of potatoes and a large number of cabbages and turnips.

These products certainly increased the health of the settlers. Various kinds of trees were planted and grew well, while peat from the peat bogs began to be used, both as a satisfactory fuel and as garden compost.

By shutting up the Labrador dogs in suitable kennels

during the summer, it became possible to increase live-stock. One of Grenfell's day helpers who began regular child welfare work attempted to solve the problem of supplying fresh milk by importing goats. These did well, but made themselves unpopular with the settlers because they did so much damage to gardens which were not fenced in. On the Mission stations, the goats were therefore replaced by cows, although numbers of goats still remained elsewhere. Lloyd George presented eight of his Yorkshire pigs to the Mission, and they did very well. Later, the Duroc-Jersey pigs proved a very suitable breed for the country. Black-faced sheep were imported from Scotland and showed themselves able to eat almost any of the Labrador wild plants. Large rabbits were also successfully raised.

The canning of fresh salmon and local berries was taken up by the fishermen's wives, and this supplied a valuable addition to the settlers' winter diet.

The instantaneous freezing of freshly caught fish made it possible to send them to distant places for marketing. They were well received. The salmon was especially popular. Queen Mary was one of the people to praise this new venture.

Labrador has immense crops of various kinds of wild berries. The blueberries were gathered and exported to America. Experiments showed that these blueberries could be cultivated and enlarged to the size of small grapes. Cranberries, yellow bake-apples and red currants all grew well.

Wild ducks and geese and their eggs were frozen or canned and kept for the winter or exported.

Because ice and snow cover Labrador for so many months of the year, and because the settlers' cottages were scattered over such a large area, there were long periods when people were unable to work, and many of them were almost destitute. Dr. Grenfell and his associates felt that doling out charity money was not only bad for these people, but not what they wanted. So gradually they were given the opportunity to make things which could be sold in other countries.

The women were taught to improve on the design and quality of the hooked mats they had always made. The men began to fashion wooden toys, animals, komatiks drawn by dog-teams, and kayaks. An ivory industry also grew up, the tusks of walruses and the teeth of whales being carved into beautiful sets of chessmen, Eskimos, seals, bears, dogs and igloos.

The Grenfell Mission had a stall at the great Imperial Exhibition at Wembley, England. It was run by a number of American volunteers who got great enjoyment out of selling model dog teams, kayaks and ivory carvings to her Majesty the Queen of England.

During a talk with King Edward VII, Grenfell was asked what he did to get policemen when he had to carry out his duties as an unpaid magistrate in Labrador. He replied, "I generally swear in an American college boy to serve your Majesty temporarily."

The Industrial Building was the old orphanage. It was leaky, shaky, unhygienic and far too small. The heating and plumbing systems were in poor condition, and the roof was so patched that it could be mended no more. Snow drifted in through the window frames.

The materials for the mats which were worked by about two thousand women of the Coast were stored here. The weaving rooms could hold only thirty looms, and many girls had to be refused employment. The wood and ivory work had to be carried out in a tiny room crowded with machinery, tools, benches, timber and half-finished articles. The waiting room to which women of the district brought their work was part of the dark and damp old kitchen, in one corner of which lay the apparatus and materials for the dyeing of the materials for the department. There was simply no money to erect new buildings.

Selling the articles produced in Labrador was difficult, for most countries charged heavy import duties. As told previously, one year some volunteers took a lorry loaded with Labrador products for sale and visited holiday resorts. At another time, Dr. Grenfell and his wife went on a combined lecture-and-selling tour in another motor truck. It was during this tour that a lady asked, "Who is that getting down from the truck?" A scornful bystander replied, "Oh, don't you know? That's the guy who wrote *Afloat on a Dustpan.*"

Shops and other buildings were rented in large towns, but often the cost of upkeep was too great, and they had to be closed down.

One venture to sell Newfoundland goods was the founding of the Dog-team Tavern in Ferrisburg, Vermont. The Grenfells rented a picturesque but dilapidated old farmhouse. Lady Grenfell appealed for help locally, and almost everything that was needed for furnishing the place, including the kitchen stove, was freely given.

Grenfell and his friends felt that the Labrador fishermen were spending far too much of their money and time in the drinking saloons of St. John's, and they were determined to build an attractive Seamen's Institute which would give the men somewhere else to spend their time.

There was much opposition to the idea, and people hinted that Grenfell was backing this venture out of personal vanity. They said, too, that such a building would simply be a white elephant. However, a hundred and seventy-five thousand dollars were raised, and the foundation stone was laid in 1911 by King George V, pressing a button in London. It all went off excellently, although the organizers admitted later that they had a man hidden under the stage, with orders to cut the rope holding the stone if the electrical apparatus failed to work.

The Institute was finally opened in the presence of the Prime Minister and many other important people. Full of joy at the success of this venture, Grenfell sailed north, only to be recalled to St. John's by a telegram. He found that the Institute funds had been misappropriated. The money was refunded, and the people concerned were punished, but permanent damage had been done to the reputation of the Institute, and the doctor suffered much anxiety and sorrow. He later said, "It was the worst time of my life."

In 1921, the little *Strathcona* was found to be badly rusted and unsafe. This was not surprising, considering that she had not only been stranded several times, but had been obliged to lie in heavy ice in harbor during the winters. She had been twice sucked down under the pressure of the ice and filled with water. Twice she had had to be sawn and dynamited out of the ice.

Lady Strathcona had the steamer reconditioned, but, unfortunately, in 1923 the craft sank in a hundred and fifty fathoms of water during a gale. The crew, who got away in the dory, were all saved.

In the same year, Grenfell bought another little steamer, which was lying up at Southampton. His friends argued that this ship, which was eighty-four feet long,

was too large to send across the Atlantic on the deck of
a liner and too small to steam across, especially as she
could carry only thirteen tons of coal.

The small ship was reconditioned and renamed *Strathcona II,* and as she lay in Southampton alongside the
S.S. Berengaria, her skipper could not resist calling on
the captain of the liner and offering to carry messages
across the Atlantic for him. The captain of the *Berengaria* peered down at the *Strathcona II* and offered to
haul her up on his davits and take her across.

The little steamer made its way via Vigo and the
Azores, and arrived at St. John's with five tons of coal
to spare.

THE REINDEER EXPERIMENT

When Dr. Grenfell began to keep records of his
patients in Labrador, he found that one in every three
deaths was due to tuberculosis and that one out of every
three native babies died in its first year. In spite of the
bracing air and plenty of sunshine, he found scurvy,
rickets and many other diseases due to insufficient food
of the right type.

All this, of course, was caused by the difficulties facing
successful farming. What was needed was milk, but,
except for a very few cattle and goats, there were no
milk-producing animals in the country.

One of the greatest problems for those people who

tried to keep farm animals was the dogs. Every family had to have half a dozen large dogs for hauling wood and traveling in the winter. It was difficult to provide these dogs with sufficient food, and they had ways of providing for themselves, especially at night. Grenfell wrote of them: "They are as resourceful as Al Capone, and require a Sherlock Holmes to bring them to justice."

Grenfell tells of a friend who sent him a beautiful white husky dog from America. The man had had it since it was a puppy, and a photograph showed it basking in the sun by a lovely brook in New England. Grenfell's friend had written a story for children about this dog, and wanted it to end its days serving humanity in a medical mission.

The morning after its arrival, one of Grenfell's biggest dogs was found dead in the dog pen. The next day, another dog was found dead. The staff now began to suspect the innocent-looking white husky and moved him into a pen by himself. There were no more deaths.

Later, he escaped from his pen one night, and although he looked very innocent in the morning he also looked suspiciously fat. From then on, they tried to make sure that he could not get out, but, somehow or other, he did and disappeared. He was later shot gorging himself on a neighbor's bull, which he had killed in the night.

Sometimes the huskies would hunt together in packs,

just like wolves, and they have been known to kill a large polar bear.

One of Grenfell's huskies vanished and was given up for lost. A complaint was made that a wolf was attacking and carrying off sheep in the neighborhood. A baited trap was set, and men armed with guns kept guard. The wolf came and was shot. It was Grenfell's long-lost husky.

The dogs, then, made cattle-raising very difficult.

The caribou, which were native to Labrador and Newfoundland, found their own food and did well. They could be domesticated and would mix with cattle. They could become quite affectionate. Grenfell tells of a fawn that was caught while swimming in a fjord and kept for a time on the hospital ship. It followed Grenfell everywhere, and when he went ashore, it would jump overboard and swim after him. When he returned to the ship, it would again swim after him. On shore, it followed close at his heels, and when it was shut inside a wooden fence, it would stand on its hind legs and try to climb over to him. These creatures seemed to survive all hazards until men began to shoot them, and then they had to be protected.

Grenfell once saw one of their largest husky dogs creeping up on a caribou tethered in the snow. But the stag saw him, and, as the dog leaped, the stag reared up on his hind legs and hit his assailant a blow which sent him flying head over heels. He was so hurt and surprised that he went away with his tail between his legs.

Because caribou lived so easily in the bleak region, it was thought that perhaps reindeer might be as successful. Reindeer need no shelter; they sleep comfortably in the open all the year round; they do not have to be fed, but with their sharp hoofs can dig through hard frozen snow more easily than a man can dig with a steel shovel, and they always seem to know just where to dig to find fresh moss under the snow.

Reindeer can haul sledges; their milk is rich and makes good cheese and butter. Their skins are ideal for fashioning light windproof clothing. Their meat is an excellent food, and their sinews provide efficient thread for insuring waterproof seams in canoes or wading boots. Reindeer also breed quickly.

Money was raised, and a herd of three hundred deer was bought in Lapland. The voyage across the Atlantic was held up by the need to put aboard enough moss to feed the deer. When they arrived, they were landed on the frozen sea, and, although some of them fell through the ice, not one of them was lost.

Three Lapp families came with the deer, to herd them and to teach others how it should be done. The herd did well, and between 1908 and 1913 the original three hundred had increased to one thousand five hundred, in spite of many unforeseen difficulties.

The Lapps, however, did not like the country, complaining that North Newfoundland was too cold. A raise in pay kept three of the men, but in the third season they all left.

One of the troubles was that there were no wolves to make the reindeer keep together, and the herds scattered over many miles. A high fence was needed to keep them together, but the money for this could not be raised.

The arrival of the reindeer also began endless trouble with the settlers and fishermen, who shot them for food. The Government ordered some protection, but this proved ineffective, and at times the doctor and the Mission were very unpopular when they tried to protect their reindeer by law. It is rather ironical that the very people Grenfell was trying to help were those who would not co-operate.

In 1914, when the First World War began, the native herders left, and Grenfell himself went to France. When he returned in 1917, he found only two hundred and thirty of the fifteen hundred deer. In order to save these, he asked the Canadian Government to accept them in their territory. They agreed and arranged for the care of the animals.

With a number of volunteers and the crew of the hospital steamer, Grenfell set out to catch the deer. With lariats, which none of them had ever used before, they managed to lasso and capture about a hundred and forty deer. But by this time the herd had become very excited. Some rushed into the wall of the corral and killed themselves. Another lot rushed headlong into the sea and swam gaily to a headland a mile away. Altogether, the amateur "cowboys" finally managed to capture a hundred and fifty. These were landed at Rocky Bay, in Canada.

Although the experiment did not have the success it deserved, Grenfell had proved that the country could support thousands of deer very cheaply on land that was otherwise useless.

17

❖━❖━❖━❖━❖━❖━❖━❖━❖━❖━❖━

Why Grenfell's Work
Succeeded in Labrador

ONE OF THE MOST remarkable features of Sir Wilfred Grenfell's medical missionary work in Labrador was the way in which he inspired others to come and help him.

Young men and young women of all kinds came voluntarily, at their own expense, to help. Some worked their passage, and some, when their money was exhausted, went home in order to earn more and return.

Over fourteen hundred helpers from Britain, America, and Canada came "down north," and twice as many were refused because they could not be accommodated. These young men called themselves Wops, a name formed from the initial letters of "With Out Pay." The young women were called Wopesses.

These young people had ingenious ways of raising money to pay their expenses. One young medical student told the doctor that he would be able to come again if his spaniel produced enough puppies for him to sell. A young lady raised the necessary money by painting and selling pictures. One of the teachers opened a tea-shop which specialized in doughnuts. She was able to stay in Labrador for eight years on what she earned.

Sir Wilfred said that the more he stressed the hardships of life in Labrador, the more recruits he got.

Older volunteers, too, came from the United States, Canada, Britain, Australia, and New Zealand. They included eminent professors, surgeons, engineers, architects, lawyers, teachers, nurses and many others.

The labor was often hard and difficult: reservoirs had to be built and pipes laid in ground that varied from swamp to solid rock, while mosquitoes and black flies descended in clouds on the workers all day long.

Buildings were constructed and ships unloaded. The captain of a coal ship who did not feel very sympathetic toward the young volunteers said that his cargo must be unloaded in three days. The boys did it with time to spare by working without a break. Sir Wilfred asked one young man how he had kept awake. He replied, "I didn't keep awake. I sat on the coal under the derrick, and every time the bucket came down it hit me on the head and I woke and filled it again."

Some of the volunteers even risked their lives. One dived into an ice-covered river and rescued two boys and was nearly drowned himself. Another went with Sir Wilfred in a small open boat to visit a patient. The craft had lost its mast and oars, and when Sir Wilfred went ashore in a dinghy, the young man anchored his boat offshore. He drifted away in the strong offshore breeze, but was later rescued.

Nurses often spent the winter months in isolated villages from which it was almost impossible to reach the nearest hospital. On one occasion, a nurse, in order to save a man's life, had to carry out a serious operation.

In another case, a nurse decided that a man must be transferred to the hospital if his life was to be saved. The journey was over such difficult country that dogs could not be used, so a team of men volunteered to drag the sledge. The nurse went with them, to look after the sick man. It took them five and a half days to reach the hospital. An operation was performed at once, and the man's life saved.

Grenfell tells of one sick call which, he said, lived vividly in his memory. A nurse was needed. The way was long, the wind cold, and the snow deep; nevertheless several nurses volunteered for the job, and one was chosen. The doctor arranged to transport her in a second komatik while his driver went ahead with the luggage to break the trail. The doctor found that he had lost some of his skill in wriggling a komatik at full speed down steep mountainsides through trees, and quite early in the day, he said later, they "looped the loop."

The last part of the journey lay across seven miles of sea ice in a large bay. It was getting dark, and suddenly thick fog drifted in from the sea. The travelers had a small compass, but trying to steer a course while dragging a heavy komatik over hummocky sea ice in the dark was almost impossible.

They finally saw a change in the ice which showed that they were either approaching land or the edge of the sea. They stopped their komatiks, and the doctor went ahead to explore. He found nothing and called back to the others. Their voices came to him from ahead. He was puzzled because he had told them not to move. In fact, he had gone round in a circle. He later said, "I can still hear that nurse laughing."

They finally made the shore, but turned the wrong way and found themselves tangled up in the Boiling Brooks, a place where underground springs keep holes open through the ice all winter. As they were moving ahead, there was suddenly a great *whurr! whurr!* under the doctor's feet. He was so startled that he dived, head first, into a snowdrift. It turned out that it was only a covey of white partridges that he had disturbed.

At length the trio reached a tiny cottage. The nurse slept on the bench, the doctor on the floor, and the driver on a shelf. There was hardly any room at all left for their generous host. As they boiled their kettle, they all agreed that they would not have missed the experience for ten rides in a Pullman car.

Grenfell's inspiration has survived him, and Wops and Wopesses still go out every year to Labrador to give the fine help which is as necessary today as it ever was.

The International Grenfell Association was incorporated in 1912. It was made up of representatives from the Grenfell Association of America, the Grenfell Association of Great Britain and Ireland, the New England Grenfell Association, the Grenfell Labrador Medical Mission and the Grenfell Association of Newfoundland.

Many people believed that this would not work because members would have to travel hundreds of miles, at their own expense, to attend meetings. But it did work. One of its main functions was to raise money, and from one member came the suggestion of establishing an endowment fund. Two hundred thousand pounds was raised, and this did much to relieve workers on the Labrador Coast of many of their financial anxieties.

As one might expect, things did not always go smoothly. One hard blow to Grenfell came in 1930 when a fire burned down the whole of Battle Harbour village, including the hospital which had done such excellent work for over thirty-eight years. But a new school and small hospital were soon functioning.

At times, Grenfell's work for the settlers and fishermen aroused deep and bitter enmity among such people as unscrupulous traders and the sellers of intoxicating liquor. But, as the Rev. Henry Gordon, who worked with him in Labrador for ten years, said, "He always fought with such obvious sincerity and lack of personal animosity that his opponents quite often became his firmest friends."

Sir Wilfred worked on in Labrador until he was over seventy. Then his doctor told him that he must retire because his heart could no longer stand the strain of his usual strenuous way of life.

He went to live at Kinloch House, on Lake Champlain, in the Adirondack Mountains. Although the country was very lovely, he was often homesick for the bare, rocky coast of Labrador. His colleagues at St. Anthony sent him a motorboat called the *Petrel,* but he found sailing on Lake Champlain very tame. In spite of his doctor's advice, Grenfell still insisted on lecturing for his beloved cause.

Lady Grenfell was determined to raise enough money to build a new Industrial Center in St. Anthony, to replace the old orphanage, but she did not live to see this accomplished. Her death was a sad blow to Sir Wilfred, and his friends felt that he never really recovered from it.

Lady Grenfell had asked, before she died, that her ashes should be scattered near their old home in St. Anthony, so in 1939 Sir Wilfred sailed again to St. Anthony. He was given a great welcome.

Friends of the Grenfells decided to build a new In-

dustrial Center as a memorial to Lady Grenfell, and
within a very short time they had raised all the money
necessary.

Sir Wilfred insisted on going on a medical cruise
"down north" once again. The thick fogs and rough seas
encountered reminded him of the old days.

At the end of August, 1939, Grenfell sailed for the last
time from St. Anthony. When he returned to Kinloch
House, he spent many hours at the Dog-team Tavern,
where he helped to sell Labrador goods and lectured to
visitors.

He died in the autumn of 1940.

Patricia Knapp, a schoolgirl, wrote this account of
staying with Grenfell. It was published in the International Grenfell Association magazine, *Among the
Deep Sea Fishers*:

"My mother and father had worked with Sir Wilfred
in Labrador for several years, and were, like everyone
who knew him, his devoted disciples. . . . I shall never
forget my first impression of him surrounded by people
in a crowded room. He was tall[1] and tanned, with a
slim, straight figure that belied his seventy-five years.
His smile was the sweetest I had ever seen, and his
friendly blue eyes shone and crinkled at the edges. . . .
After lunch Sir Wilfred startled the whole family by

[1] He probably seemed tall to Patricia, but in fact he was of
medium height.

insisting that I should come to visit him. . . . On the way to Charlotte, where Sir Wilfred's home is, we stopped at the Dog-team Tavern. The inn was started by Lady Grenfell, and so was very dear to Sir Wilfred's heart. . . . While I was there I met some of the volunteer workers who said they had never known a man who had so many friends. . . . The next morning . . . I was awakened by an eerie howling. Terrified at first, I was much relieved to hear Sir Wilfred saying, 'Sing, Kimmie boy, sing.' Kim was Sir Wilfred's cocker spaniel. The night before I had watched him beg, roll over, play dead, take a handkerchief from Sir Wilfred's pocket, and do any number of remarkable tricks, but when I heard him sing, I, like Sir Wilfred, was sure of his super-animal qualities.

"Before we started breakfast Sir Wilfred read, as always, out of a book which his wife had compiled just before she died. He said it not only started him out right for the day, but that it made him feel nearer to his wife. Then we knelt before our chairs while Sir Wilfred said a prayer. After breakfast we all went to church. It was a small church in which every voice counted. Sir Wilfred's was loud, sincere, and a bit off key. . . .

"Sunday night was the part of my whole visit I enjoyed most. We spent the entire evening together in his study. It was then that I learned what a true Christian he was. He said . . . that to follow Christ was an invitation never to get weary of being alive, and that Christ lived with those who worked. He told me how he read his Bible, marked with his own observations, and then often gave it away to some one who begged for it. . . . I learned of his great longing for his wife. He read to me in his beautiful voice and told me stories of Labrador, which he felt was his real home. . . .

"I shall never forget him, nor will anyone who has ever shaken his hand. I cannot believe he is dead, because his spirit is so alive. As he said, 'You live on even after death, in the hearts of those who love you.' "

Julian Duguid, the traveler, once met Sir Wilfred on board ship, and said of him:

"For a week . . . his face astonished, held me. I had never experienced such power. . . . He had an aura of peace and strength which could be felt across the smoking-room. With hundreds of strangers present, and my own back turned, I could tell directly he entered. . . . It was enough to be near him. He refreshed by being himself."

The Rev. Henry Gordon said about him in an address given in 1956:

"I would like to single out three . . . qualities which always made a particular impression upon me.

"The first was his intense love of life. Grenfell literally bubbled over with his exuberance of spirits. His energy and enthusiasm knew no bounds. This made him at times a most exhausting person to live with. I remember one occasion on which I was a passenger on board his Mission ship *Strathcona*. We spent the whole day from dawn to sunset loading wood for one of his hospitals. After this Grenfell insisted on discussing some new and, to us, hare-brain scheme, which lasted till 2 A.M. Then, just when we were sunk in blissful slumber at about 6 A.M., there was the doctor as fresh as a daisy calling us to get going as *he* hadn't any time to waste.

"A second great quality of Grenfell's was his simple, almost childlike trust and confidence. It was this that freed him from even the slightest semblance of fear or thought of danger. For these we who were his friends were often wont to chide him, for what seemed to us just sheer recklessness. But it made no difference. He really did believe that he was immortal till his work was done.

"A friend of his earlier days related the following incident. They were out together in a small sailing boat on the North Sea when a gale got up and there was considerable danger of their boat being swamped. At last his friend could stand it no longer, and suggested that they should put back into port. 'Why?' replied Grenfell. 'What are you worrying about? The Lord will look after us.' And that was typical of Grenfell's faith. Call it childish or irrational if you will, but it worked. But Grenfell would never have survived for more than a few years if there had not been some one looking after him. And it was perhaps natural that this simple faith in God should have found an echo in his attitude towards his fellowmen. It wasn't that he was blind to people's faults, but that he just could not believe that anybody was past redemption. This was often a source of considerable embarrassment to his directors when at last he had to consent to some kind of organization behind his work. At any time he might turn up with a crew of scalliwags whom he was convinced were capable of reformation. Often enough he proved right, for I know of several men who were able to regain their self-respect through Grenfell's faith in them.

"The third . . . quality . . . was his peculiar gift of being able to inspire us with his own ideals. He had an especial magnetism for young people, as, indeed, he still has today, years after his death. For many years all his workers in Labrador, with the exception of a few trained assistants, were volunteers, and so keen were people to give their services that many of them had to be refused. To visit one of his mission stations in those early years of his work was to find a situation that would have rejoiced the heart of even the most pronounced socialist. It reminded one of those lines of Kipling's descriptive of the rush of volunteers for the Boer War, 'Duke's son, cook's son, son of a millionaire.' But it must not be imagined that to work with Grenfell was a pleasant holiday picnic. As I have already intimated, he never spared himself and he never spared anyone else. Nothing was too good or too hard in his Master's service. In some ways this was perhaps Grenfell's greatest achievement. For although there have been many men who have left their mark on the world, few could have been such an abundant source of inspiration to their fellow-creatures, and no better evidence of this can be found than in the way in which those who carry on his great work today reflect his spirit and share his ideals."

Sir Henry Richards, Chairman of the Council of the Grenfell Association of Great Britain and Ireland and the close friend of Sir Wilfred for many years, gives us in the following words perhaps the clearest picture of his character and the reason for the great success of his work in Labrador:

"Grenfell was in many aspects of his work and character a strange paradox. A visionary, impatient of detail and of regulation, who, nevertheless, could mold his dreams into realities and his thoughts into action. A speaker, haphazard and diffuse, destitute of any of the arts of the orator, but able to move and inspire great audiences by words which in their simplicity and ingenuousness rose yet to a lofty eloquence. No deep thinker or learned scholar, yet he swayed the mind and affected the attitude of great seats of learning and of men distinguished in every field of thought and action. At times a perpetual boy, irresponsible, wilful, and arbitrary, who bent men to his will, and carried through with system and shrewdness great and complicated enterprises. To what did he owe his amazing influence apart from his personal magnetism? I think the answer is clear; it was to the transparent sincerity and simplicity of his faith, to his direct and unhesitating interpretation into action of the spirit of his Master.

"When I first knew him over fifty years ago [this was written in 1947] at the London Hospital, at Oxford, and on the North Sea, he had for his contemporaries all the attraction of a fine athlete and daring seaman, but he had something more. Round him there was a radiance of strength and purity which turned those who knew him from evil to good, and from hesitancy to confidence, which inspired them with his own indignation of wrong, his courage to rebuke vice, his love for the oppressed, the poverty-stricken, the sick, and the unhappy. His high ends he approached with a serious resolve, but ever with cheeriness and humor and good fellowship. He was indeed the Happy Warrior, the Good Companion, marching to his Journey's End. He lived and labored to make the material world around him a better and happier place, and yet his real life was lived elsewhere. Often he gave the impression of a mere sojourner and pilgrim seeking another country, a heavenly one and a surer Haven."

In the summer of 1941, Grenfell's ashes were scattered,

like those of his wife, in St. Anthony, and crowds of his old friends came to pay him their last respects.

On August 4, 1942, there was a great gathering at St. Anthony to celebrate the fiftieth anniversary of Grenfell's landing on the Coast. Messages came from King George VI and President Roosevelt, and a memorial tablet was unveiled.

Sir Wilfred, the man of action, who escaped death so narrowly on so many occasions, and who, if there were two alternatives, always chose the more adventurous, summed up his attitude to life in the following words:

"We are not here to be safe. We must have faith and take risks. Life is not meant to be easy and humdrum. Life is a challenge, and we are so made as to respond, for we are the sons of God. . . . I would not have lost the opportunity of going to Labrador for anything."